REVELATION

Understanding the Age

Kevin Hartley

ISBN 979-8-88644-101-7 (Paperback)
ISBN 979-8-88644-102-4 (Digital)

All scriptures, unless otherwise stated, are taken from
the King James Version of the Holy Bible.

Covenant Books
11661 Hwy 707
Murrells Inlet, SC 29576
www.covenantbooks.com

For My Wife Oneida
Whose love and patience,
care and assistance
made this book possible.

CONTENTS

PREFACE

Commentaries on the book of Revelation have saturated the Christian book market for the last two centuries. There is little doubt that another such commentary will garner little attention amongst those interested in the study. Yet, this commentary is a bit unique. First, it is Amillenial, and as such, few commentaries exist from this vantage. Second, it is Reformed, and few Reformed commentaries on the book of Revelation exist. Third, it is written with a thesis in mind, as it approaches the book from the situational perspective given by the Lord's directive to the apostle John at the close of the biblical canon. Last, it is not overtly technical. While Greek studies, when necessary, are conducted, the majority of the commentary focuses upon the reading and interpretation of the book itself. Thus, the book is better classified as a *reader's commentary*, much like those of the Reformed Expository Commentary series.

Great weight was put upon the scholarship and insights of two authors, William Hendriksen and James Ramsey: James Ramsey, a nineteenth century graduate of Princeton Seminary, a pastor and missionary, his work in Revelation did much to unlock the hidden intricacies and designs behind the first 11 chapters of the book. Ramsey's findings were complimented by the exquisite scholarship of William Hendriksen, a 20th century New Testament scholar, graduate of Princeton, and early opponent of dispensationalism. Together, their insights opened up some of the more complex passages of the book of Revelation. The reader is encouraged to investigate their works for further study.

It is this author's hope that many such commentaries from this biblical and orthodox view of the book of Revelation will follow. For just as is stated in this commentary the study of Revelation is essential for the church in this present age. Being able to understand the book and put it to use in the Christian's life is vital. Pre-millennial dispensationalism is the loudest voice in the evangelical world today. Movies are filmed. Books are written. Seminars and conferences are held. Radio programs and television programs fill the airways leading people to imagine some impending Armageddon, a rising up of an antichrist, and a rapture that scripture never teaches. Vast resources are spent teaching the masses that Israel as a nation is central to God's plan today, even though scripture is clear that no such distinction exists in our day. You cannot turn on a supposed *Christian* radio program without someone divining the times and the signs based upon events in the Middle East and supposed literal signs indicated in the book of Revelation. It is time to stop the madness. Let's put Revelation back where it belongs, at the end of God's remarkable book, and then back in the church instructing us how to live in this troublesome age. *Soli Deo Gloria*

INTRODUCTION

The book of Revelation is key to understanding the mind of God in the present age. It is the blueprint for comprehending this world in which we live. God has divided history in two: the previous age before Christ, the present age of Christ; the age anticipating His incarnation, and the age preceding His return; the age before His reign, the age of His reign; the age before the kingdom come, the age of the kingdom come. As this age is about the reign of Christ having come, as it is about His conquering, subduing, and completing the sovereign eternal plan of redemption and glory foreordained by the eternal godhead, Revelation then stands as the book key to the design of God for this, the final age. It is the portrait of God's grand scope and design for this age, the compendium of redemptive history in these last days. Without Revelation's insight, the world is confusing, often frustrating, even dispiriting, leaving our Lord's bride absent hope and certainty. With Revelation's glorious insights, we come to see the divine plan of the ages and the manner in which our Lord is advancing that plan. The last days began long ago, and they are advancing; therefore it is essential that the Lord's children have a clear understanding of our Lord's divine will in this present evil age. Our Lord placed the book of Revelation at the end of His book, and rightly so, as it is the final anthology of the Lord's eternal design in this created order. It is the last word from heaven in this the last age.

For most of this age, the church has been deprived of the illuminating insights of this book, either through neglect, trepidation, or misconception. The church has been robbed of the most glorious insights and benefits intended by our Lord for His people in this last of books. Many have simply considered the book of no value or canonical significance; doubting its worth or value for the church, they have merely left it unopened and sitting upon the shelf. Some have feared the seeming complexities and difficulties of the book and have timidly simply left it untouched. Others have so misconstrued and wrongly interpreted the book that they have done great harm and damage to the Word of God and its truth, misleading and misdirecting those under their care. It is far time for the Lord's people to reclaim the most precious of books, to recover the insights most vital to living in this age, seeking its blessed encouragement, and receiving from God that most glorifying gift of this age, granted to us by the sovereign grace and will of our God. Our Lord gave it to us; He intended us to read it and know it, not to ignore it, and certainly not to fear it nor be deceived by its misuse and misinterpretation. It, as all Scripture, is given to instruct, direct, reprove, correct, and embolden our Lord's beloved children so that He might be greatly glorified, and we, the church, comforted in these last days. As Paul so succinctly wrote, "All scripture is given by inspiration of God, and is profitable for doctrine, for reproof, for correction, for instruction in righteousness: That the man of God may be perfect, throughly furnished unto all good works" (2 Tim. 3:16f). Revelation should be as useful as any other book of scripture. The fact that it was placed last in our canon makes it even more essential and vital for living in our day. It is essential that we know it so that we might persevere and endure in these last evil days.

Perhaps the greatest impediment to rightly understanding the book of Revelation today is the rise of dispensationalism in the last century and a half. With its faulty hermeneutic and broad popularity, it has left many believing in far-off fairytales and myths, wrongly dividing the Word of God and leading vast numbers down the path of one man's imagination. It is not the purpose of this book to refute dispensationalism, nor every erroneous attempt to interpret Revelation; however, the detrimental impact of dispensationalism on the understanding and use of this book since the mid-nineteenth century demands its refutation.

Essentially, dispensationalism's error lies in its misinterpretation of the book's overall design. The book is not intended for a far-off age. It is a book intended for this present age. Consider how counterintuitive it would be for God to design a second testament, comprised of four gospels, one history book, and twenty-one letters to churches and individuals from the first century. If this were the case, and Revelation was merely for a distant, far-off age, then God left the church of this age without insight and understanding of so vast a period of time. God has not left the church blind to this age, but as John said, Revelation contains insights and understanding for the present age, writing, "Blessed is he that readeth, and they that hear the words of this prophecy, and keep those things which are written therein: for the time is at hand" (Rev. 1:3). Yet a more central error lies behind dispensationalism's misconception of the book: it has misinterpreted and misunderstood the place of Israel in redemptive history. A proper understanding of Israel's place in redemptive history is key to understanding the book of Revelation.

That said, let us be clear, the book of Revelation is the key book necessary to conclude Scripture; it is the capstone upon the inerrant, inspired, divine work of impeccable glory. It is given to illuminate and summarize the work of our reigning Lord in this present age. It explains the fullness of the godhead's work in creation. It finishes the story. Its central theme is the final, culmination of the eternal plan brought forth in redemption and judgment. As such, it is both an epistle and a book of prophecy. It is the book that outlines the grand scheme of God from the day of Pentecost until the return of our Lord. It is self-interpreting on its own, as much of its metaphors and allegories are internally defined, as well as it being self-interpreting canonically as a whole, as it, along with various prophetic images of old and the allusions of the past, is given to provide ample information to decode its symbolic truths. Put at the end, it serves as the final and definite revelation of our Lord for the people of God in these final days.

Consider, Revelation is neither chronological nor literal; it is thematic. Overall, it can be divided into two parts, the epistolary portion and the prophetic portion. Yet a more natural and inherent division comes from the text itself as the book is naturally divided into three principal parts. The first part shows the apostle John receiving a present view of Christ amidst His churches at the end of the first century. This view is from the vantage point of heaven. Christ gives it the designation *the things which were*, indicating it is that first seen by the apostle. The second section contains seven epistles given to the seven churches of Asia Minor, which are written to by John on behalf of the Lord, also occurring at the end of the first century. Of this, Christ applies the designation of *the things which are*. And last, there is that prophetic part of the book that presents the divine work of our Lord in this present age. This is designated by our Lord as *the things which shall shortly come to pass*. The phrase itself argues against an interlude of time, as Christ says it must *shortly come to pass*. The things within this vision are those that began in John's day and will end at the return of Christ.

This last designation of time, called *the things which shall shortly come to pass*, is set within the construct of a creation week. It is divided into the likeness of seven days, in order to demonstrate the creative sovereign work of God to be completed unto perfection in this age, just as was done in that first week. It is symbolic, metaphorical, representative, a grand view of this age and the Lord's sovereign work within it. Overall, these are the grand divisions of the book, which Christ sets down with these words to John, "Write the things which thou hast seen, and the things which are, and the things which shall be hereafter" (Rev. 1:19). This central division of Revelation establishes the three principal parts of the book.

Beneath the third division is a second division of three parts. As the overarching purpose of the book is to embolden the church in this present age with the knowledge of the Lord's sovereign design, this last division makes up the majority of the prophecy itself; in fact, one might say the former part is epistolary and this latter part prophetic. The prophetic part is in itself like unto a whole. Thus, it is set down in the form of a creative week, where this present age is likened unto God's first creation; it is set down in the construct of seven, ending in a perfect and completed work, a final sabbath rest.

As in the first creative work where all things came forth from the divine will, so these revelations always proceed from the throne of God; as such, they indicate the sovereign, eternal, work of the divine will. With the first age gone, and Christ our Lord having ascended to be seated at the right hand of the Father, we see Him now governing and conducting the will of the Father as set forth from before the ages began. Christ the Lamb is the Lord enthroned who has been given authority by which He carries out the foreordained divine plan of the Father. He is seen as a conquering King and Lamb, who prevails by His blood. All the while the world and all the fallen created order are allied with the devil against our King and His elect. The elect of God are also known as the true Israel of God, the woman, and His bride, with whom He is bound by an eternal covenant of grace, to redeem, deliver, and subdue her foes so that they might be as one in the end. It is this portion of Revelation, the final part, which is of such great use to the bride of Christ in this present age.

The following will be a study of this present age, as set forth to us in the book of Revelation. But as has been shown, it can also be said to be a study of the plan of God in this present age. It is set forth in the final words of our Lord, meant for us, and designed to be understood and employed by us so that we might persevere and endure unto the end. This study will seek exegetical certainty. It will endeavor to provide necessary clarity and insight for the reader. It will be an endeavor to instruct the reader in doctrinal certainty and the useful application of the text. But most of all, it will make every effort to be doxologically designed, as it is our central calling in all that we do, to seek to glorify God and Him alone. For that which we seek to understand is the hidden, mysterious wonders of our Lord's eternal covenantal work on a scale so grand and marvelous that the finite mind is at a loss. Yet with the Lord's grace and allowance, we shall seek to know Him in all His sovereign and supreme designs and manifestations, accentuating the absolute inability of man to achieve his own ends, and our absolute impotency in our salvation and deliverance; or to put it simply, it will be a study set to punctuate its effort with this phrase, "Soli Deo Gloria." Still, as with all scripture, it shall be Christocentric, for all things revolve around our Lord and His glory.

CHAPTER 1

INTRODUCTION

The key to the interpretation of the book of Revelation is found in chapter 1. The first chapter provides us with much of what is necessary to properly interpret and understand the book. In the first chapter, we find the canonical genre of the book itself. Here, the book is set down in two categories, it is an epistle, and it is prophecy; thus, we can expect the material in this book to have epistolary relevance as well as prophetic significance. As a letter, Revelation has its primary use for those present in John's final days. It was that revelation given to those suffering from persecution at the eclipse of the apostolic age. Yet like all New Testament letters, it has bearing and application to Christians throughout this age. The epistles of chapter 2 and 3 have much to say to the church and to Christians in these last days. Like all scripture, they provide the believer throughout this age with direction, reproof, correction, and instruction in righteousness, to the end of our maturation in Christ.

In chapter 1, we also find the book's historic setting, which is the backdrop to the epistolary portion of the book. This insight provides context to the book's content. We shall hear of John's plight at the end of the first century AD; we shall hear of his predicament on Patmos and his enduring hope for the Lord's return in glory. We shall be instructed in living, enduring, and striving in righteousness as pilgrims and sojourners in a hostile, foreign, and fallen world. We shall seek to be afforded the grace of God's Spirit to grow in faith so that we might live and endure in this present evil age. We shall learn key and principal doctrines about our God and about His person. Furthermore, we shall even be given insight into the scheme of God in both His eternal redemptive covenant and judgment. In this way, Revelation will function as any other New Testament epistle, set within the backdrop of its historic context.

Yet as it has been said, Revelation also is prophetic. In fact, most of Revelation fits this category. Like all prophecy, it shall serve to anticipate the future. The book shall look forward to the day of the Lord. It will warn the stubborn and adjure the faithful. In doing so, it shall employ imagery and metaphor, all to illustrate the Lord's grand scheme for the final age of this world. This is nothing new, as imagery and metaphor are common to the prophetic form. Revelation shall richly draw upon the canon's former prophetic works. That which is seen will represent that which shall be. From John's gospel, we see that John already has an inclination for metaphor, so it should come as no surprise to see him continue with this form. Like all prophecy, Revelation shall employ dreams and visions of things that represent things that shall be. Together then, Revelation as both an epistolary and prophetic book will prove to be a book of grand complexities, rich with vital importance, of most necessary use for the church in this age.

Chapter 1, in addition to giving us canonical insight, also provides us with the scope of the material found in the book; Revelation is for the present age. Twice the book is shown in the first chapter to designate its contents for this present age. Scripture is clear that this is the last age, that we are in the last days, and that these last days span from the days of the apostles until the return of our Lord. When Peter stood and explained the events occurring at Pentecost, he quoted Joel's words, saying, "But this is that which was spoken by the prophet Joel; And it shall come to pass in the last days, saith God, I will pour out of my Spirit upon all flesh: and your sons and your daughters shall prophesy, and your young men shall see visions, and your old men shall dream dreams" (Acts 2:16f). As Joel prophesied and Peter indicated, Pentecost was the beginning of these last days, which shall last until when Christ returns, upon which they shall end. Hebrews begins with this affirmation, saying, "God, who at sundry times and in divers manners spake in time past unto the fathers by the prophets, Hath in these last days spoken unto us by his Son" (Heb. 1:1f). Scripture is unequivocal on this matter, these are the last days; there were the former days before Christ appeared, and now these are the last days from which we eagerly await His return. There are but two ages biblically and history is divided this way; God's eternal redemptive plan spans two ages.

Thus, as Revelation is the book given to explain these last days, it uses language appropriate to this design. The parameter is set down in chapter 1 with the phrases *shortly come to pass* and *for the time is at hand.* Both phrases indicate that the content of the book is not for a distant future, but for this present age. *At hand* is right before us, so near that it is at the ready grasp. When Christ said, "The kingdom of heaven is at hand," He spoke of it having drawn near in Him. It had arrived; it had come. It was just over the horizon, as close as He was to those to whom He spoke. It was not some distant, long-away age; rather, it was as though one could touch it. Understand that it would do hermeneutical violence to attempt to put that which is *at hand* far off in an age yet to come. *At hand* speaks to the immediacy of those things to be revealed. Added to the phrase *at hand* is the phrase *shortly come to pass.* The literal reading of the phrase ἃ δεῖ γενέσθαι ἐν τάχει, which could be rendered *that which must come immediately*, implies immediacy. This phrase speaks to both the urgency and the imminence of these things to be revealed. It also speaks to their enduring design. Many would have us believe that chapter 4 onward in the book is for some far-away distant age; however, the parameters established by our Lord in this first chapter will not support such a conclusion. For the things found in this book are *at hand* and shall *Immediately* come to pass. Revelation is for the here and now.

Consider this, if this book were not predominantly a synopsis of this age, then God has left us nothing for this age; we would be left with nothing beyond the epistles for our help. The epistles contain little insight into the grand design and purpose of our God in this present age. If we were to accept the conclusions of those who have relegated this book's use to a future age and their assumption that this present age is nothing more than a parenthesis in God's true redemptive plan, then this age would be but one of insignificance and a trivial parenthesis. If this is the case, then God has done the church of this age a grand disservice; for what would we have to explain this age? What would be ours for encouragement and faith? We would be left with disillusionment and despair.

However, God has not left us void of His word in these last days. Revelation is the key to this age; it is that necessary insight given to illuminate the plan behind the chaos of this age. It is the book given to comfort us, to encourage us, and to instruct us in these last days. It is the book that is so very necessary for us to know so that we do not lose heart. What God did in the law and the prophets for the saints of old He has done most magnificently in the epistolary canon of the New Testament. He has finished His special revelation with a crown of its own, Revelation, which is the final piece of the puzzle. Our Lord has given us the key to a full and perfect insight into His sovereign will and plan drawn out in two grand ages. He has given us the insight and instruction necessary to persevere until that day of Christ's return. The first chapter of Revelation demonstrates and affirms the immediacy and relevancy of this book for the here and now. Revelation is the unveiling of our risen Lord's final act, it is the culmination of God's glorious design, and it is *at hand*; the time is now.

As we have seen, the first chapter of Revelation provides us with the scope and genre of its content; here also it has provided us with its hermeneutic. Nothing is as it seems; everything is symbolic, representative, figurative, and while mysterious, to be interpreted and understood. It is Christ Himself that establishes this principal of interpretation, as He is first to interpret the meaning of those things seen by the apostle John. The Lord reveals that stars are not stars and candlesticks are not candlesticks; they are figures for that which they represent. Revelation 1, like the whole of the book itself, is rich with allusions and figures, all of which have meanings that are to be found in what those images represent. Often, the Lord or an angel shall give explanation to those things seen. At other times, scripture itself will provide the insight needed in passages found outside the book itself.

When explanations are not given, past prophecies and biblical types shall provide the insight needed to understand the things seen. What John sees in this book are images of things represented. Often these images are layered, overlapping, multifaceted, and complex. They are images that represent truths that are to be understood. Nothing John sees is to be taken to represent the reality of that which it represents.

One example is found in chapter 1, where the glorious Son of God is seen with a sharp two-edged sword protruding from His mouth. This we know: Jesus does not have a sword protruding obtusely from His mouth; the image is not what it appears to be, but it represents something *about* our Lord. The sword represents the Word of God, its power, and might, as is found in Hebrews 4:12, where we read, "For the word of God is quick, and powerful, and sharper than any two-edged sword, piercing even to the dividing asunder of soul and spirit, and of the joints and marrow, and is a discerner of the thoughts and intents of the heart." That it comes from His mouth affirms what John says, when he writes, "And the Word became flesh" (John 1:14). Christ is the word and by His word He makes war. This example from the first chapter shows us that things seen by John are metaphors and symbols and not literally to be understood, and to interpret them in any other way than the way they were intended is to misinterpret the text itself. John employed such images and metaphors in the writing of his Gospel; here he but continues to employ metaphors and images to represent the truth. Christ's appearance is telling; it is not so much what He looks like, but what that image represents. His glorious image speaks of His wisdom, His incarnate work unto our perseverance and endurance; it speaks of His righteousness and holiness, His majesty and divinity. The images we see in Revelation are to be interpreted not misinterpreted. Revelation is a book of figures and images, metaphors, and types; nothing in Revelation is as it seems.

We also find that Revelation is a book interspersed with the shadows of the Old Covenant. The appearance of Christ is likened unto the high priest. The place in which He walks is like unto the Temple that once stood on earth. The backdrop of the images seen in Revelation are the antitypes of those things once constructed in the previous age of shadows. That which under the Old Covenant was made visible on Earth is now realized in heaven. These will be the backdrop of the book of Revelation. The candlesticks, the altar of incense, the golden censor, the ark of the covenant, all of these are emblems found in Revelation that serve as the setting from which all things proceed. In the temple above the Lord reigns and brings to pass all that which comes to pass among us here below. The setting of this book is heavenly, the stage where those things decreed above are brought to pass is on the Earth below. From the heavenly tabernacle comes the directives of the Almighty to bring to pass that which is done below.

The illustrative history of Israel in the previous age is also interwoven into the tapestry of Revelation. We find allusions to the Exodus, to Babylon, to Joseph and Israel, all of which are employed as backdrops to complete the picture of the book. Revelation does not stand alone, and as it serves as the final chapter of that book begun so long ago, we find that it employs facets of form and nuance from the various revelations of God's special will through the ages. Revelation is the capstone of all scripture, and as such, it uses scripture as its warp and woof. Interwoven throughout it are shadows and figures of the Old Covenant. They once so perfectly formed a remarkable image of our Lord and His salvific glory. Now, they are used again to illustrate that which the Lord is bringing to pass. Long ago, He purposed to save us and now He is set to finish that work. As the Lord finishes this mighty work, He moves the apostle to finish it with one final wondrous tapestry of sovereign glory, employing aspects of all of scripture and history to complete this work. And most of all, in the end, Christ stands alone.

Revelation is a book of hope and encouragement. It was given to embolden and encourage the church at the end of the Apostolic age, and it remains a book chiefly for our encouragement. It was penned by the apostle John from Patmos during his exile there under the emperor Domitian, around the year AD 96. This date is not to be refuted; scholarship that has attempted to predate the book prior to this date is biased, seeking to affirm a faulty hermeneutic by denouncing what is historically certain. Beyond the internal evidence, external proof has been incontrovertible since Irenaeus, the earliest recorded witness and disciple of Polycarp, the direct disciple of John himself, who wrote,

> We will not, however, incur the risk of pronouncing positively as to the name of Antichrist; for if it were necessary that his name should be distinctly revealed in this present time, it would have been announced by him who beheld the apocalyptic vision. For that was seen not very long time since, but almost in our day, towards the end of Domitian's reign. (Irenaeus, *Against Heresies*, v. xxx. 3)

Revelation is set in a time when persecution was at its cruelest, the apostolic host was all but gone, and John stood alone; there was an undeniable need for insight into the Lord's will that the church might not be dismayed. Revelation provided just this material. It was the final book of the canon, God's final word in that day, for those that feared the kingdom was all but lost and those that believed all hope was gone. Revelation was for those that would soon see the last living witness of the risen Lord perish; it was the book necessary for the perseverance of the saints through faith in that day. And just as Revelation was essential to the church of that day, so is it equally vital for our day. It is the key to living in the post-apostolic world of warfare and persecution, a key that John and the church were given in a time of great tribulation necessary for us and them to endure life in a hostile world.

One final insight afforded us in the first chapter of Revelation necessary for rightly interpreting the book is understanding the central theme of the book itself, which is God's sovereignty. God is sovereignly establishing His kingdom in this world through the conquest and judgment of this world. This is the central theme of the book from the start to the finish. The past age was the age anticipating the coming of our Lord and His kingdom. This age is the age of our Lord reigning. His kingdom having come, it grows, and as it grows it advances, and as it advances the world is subdued. The spoils of Christ's conquest include peoples from all nations, being made one with Israel, Israel of the promise, so that both Jew and Gentile, together they are the true Israel of God. This is the age of light infusing into the darkness. It is the age of the repeal and ebb of Satan's reign and authority. It is the age of our Lord's covenant glory magnifying His redemptive mercy and vindicating justice. It is the age of the Lamb victorious, who rules from the throne of heaven, in Jerusalem above, having done away with all types and shadows, He rides forth conquering and to conquer. This is the book of God's vindication and the world's judgment, it is the book of Satan's demise and end, it is the book of the final ingathering of all God's elect, and the glorious conquest and splendor of the Lord of lords and King of kings. This is the book of Revelation, the book that can no longer be left upon the shelf, which must become the book most cherished by us all, recovered from all the foolish imaginations and misinterpretations of old, restored to its proper place, so that the Lamb's people might presently reign in Him with all hope and courage in this present evil age.

Yet we would be remiss to neglect mention of the first chapter of Revelation's most vital point, it is the book of the Revelation of *Jesus Christ*. It reveals His glory. It reveals His majesty. It, as all of scripture, is Christocentric. He is seen exalted and enthroned, high above all principalities, might and dominion. He is seen as King of kings and Lord of lords. He is God of God and Man of Man. He is the central figure of the book, He is the central theme of all scripture, and to fail to read Revelation without Christ central to it is to fail to rightly interpret the book. He is our Lord, who is set before us to see, to behold, and to worship, and in Revelation, we see Him exalted in all His glory and splendor. Revelation read without Christ central to its every design is to fail to understand the true glory of this book. In the end, Christ alone stands on High. We see Him who has been victorious and all by His blood. This is after all the proper title of the book, given at the start, where it titles itself *the Revelation of Jesus Christ*. Paul said to the Colossians,

> He is the image of the invisible God, the
> firstborn of every creature: For by him were

all things created, that are in heaven, and that are in earth, visible and invisible, whether they be thrones, or dominions, or principalities, or powers: all things were created by him, and for him: And he is before all things, and by him all things consist. And he is the head of the body, the church: who is the beginning, the firstborn from the dead; that in all things he might have the preeminence. For it pleased the Father that in him should all fulness dwell; And, having made peace through the blood of his cross, by him to reconcile all things unto himself; by him, I say, whether they be things in earth, or things in heaven.

Like Colossians, Revelation is most of all Christocentric. It is the glory of the Son of God. In the end, we must see Him.

Chapter 1 Analysis

With that said, let us turn to the interpretation of Revelation chapter 1. The chapter contains three divisions; a general introduction (v. 1–3), an epistolary introduction (v. 4–8), and a prefatory vision given the apostle anticipating the letters to the seven churches to follow (v. 9–20). As is common to the book itself, all visions and prophecies are preceded by a look to the heavenly throne. The throne of God sets the stage for the action that follows; everything always proceeds from the sovereign will and initiation of the Lord. This first vision also provides the framework for the interpretation of all subsequent visions; they are set within that which is the antitype of the old earthly temple and are given direction and interpretation by those entrusted with explaining the vision to the apostle. With this, we shall examine the chapter's content.

The general introduction in verses 1–3 serves to establish the divine origin of the book. It is the revelation of Jesus Christ, that which has been entrusted to Him by the Father, for the purpose of making known that which shall *shortly come to pass* which is *at hand.* This is no vision of another age, another time, or another future dispensation; this is the revelation of Jesus Christ for this present age. It was then applicable, it is now being made known and accomplished, and it is certain to be completed in this present time. These two modifiers provide the time stamp of this book; it is for these last days, this latter age while the former days had their prophecy and word from heaven, so our days has this prophecy and word from heaven. Thus, it is said to "bear record of the word of God, and the testimony of Jesus Christ." It was entrusted to the Lord, dispersed to His servants, and sent and signified to the apostle John. It was given at the close of the apostolic age. It is intended to be declared, understood, and employed by the Lord's people, as it says, "Blessed is he that readeth, and they that hear the words of this prophecy, and keep those things which are written therein." Thus, it is criminal to relegate this book to a future time; it is for our use now. It explains the Lord's will and work for us now, for as it says, *"The time is at hand."* This general introduction serves to incite the reader to read, to understand, and to reap the benefits of the word of the Lord for our living in these last of days.

How John must have relished the receipt of this revelation. It must have warmed his heart to be afforded the privilege of revealing that made known to him on Patmos in those days. It had been so long since he had seen the Lord, nearly fifty-eight years, and now at last he would see Him again. But not as before, for now He would see Him as he never had, enthroned, glorified, magnified in all His glory, one with the Father and the Spirit, set to make known that which for so long had been concealed. As the book of Revelation opens with this grand introduction, history and providence are interrupted by this declaration,

> The Revelation of Jesus Christ, which God
> gave unto him, to shew unto his servants things
> which must shortly come to pass; and he sent and
> signified it by his angel unto his servant John:
> Who bare record of the word of God, and of the

testimony of Jesus Christ, and of all things that he saw. Blessed is he that readeth, and they that hear the words of this prophecy, and keep those things which are written therein: for the time is at hand.

John was surely blessed to receive this from his Lord.

Note that a blessing is attached to Revelation that does not directly accompany any other book of scripture. A blessing is added for those that read and hear the things contained within but added to this is the admonition to "*keep those things that are written therein.*" For the Word of God is not merely to be read but kept. These three participles of verse 3 in the Greek, translated as reading, hearing, and keeping, remind us of the vital importance of this prophecy's use for our living in this present age. It says that those that are incessantly engaged in the review and use of this book are blessed. How? By reading, hearing, and keeping. Why? It says the reason for the blessing is due to that which is read, heard, and kept being *at hand.* A beatitude accompanies those engaged in the use of this prophecy. Μακάριος is that word Christ our Lord employed in the beatitudes. It speaks to our happiness and contentment not in this world, but in the glorious realm of our Lord's reign. In the kingdom of heaven, we are called blessed. Here, those that are found reading, hearing, and heeding the words of this prophecy are called blessed. Happy are those that understand the Lord's will and work in this present age. Happy are those that observe His sovereign glory and providence advancing unto His conquest of this world and our foes in this present age. We are called *blessed* because these things are *at hand.* They are here, now they are transpiring, now they are coming to pass, and as they do, we rejoice to see our Lord's will done in heaven and on Earth. We are happy because it is the Lord's will that has, is, and shall come to pass in this the last of days.

Next, the general introduction is followed by an epistolary introduction. With three specific introductions, Revelation has several layers to its beginning. Like the other letters of the New Testament, so this letter has equal historical context. Verses 4–8 are the introduction to the seven letters to be sent to the seven churches of Asia Minor. However, this epistolary introduction is nothing like John's other introductions found in his three short epistles. There, John was cryptic; here, he is direct. The apostle John introduces himself, which he failed to do explicitly in any of his other writings, and even here he adopts an epistolary preface foreign to his other three letters, but this is intentional. For this is not *his* letter to the churches; it is the *Lord Jesus Christ's* epistle to the churches and that of the Holy Spirit, here identified as the seven spirits before the throne of God. No other New Testament letter claims to be the direct product of the Lord and His Spirit. While all letters bear divine inspiration, this one is unique in that the apostle is a mere messenger entrusted with the letter composed by Christ and the Spirit. John is merely the scribe of heaven. Revelation then has this unique to its design. Like the prophets of old, John is merely the vessel foreordained to prophesy the word of the Lord. So while it is a common epistolary introduction, it is unique in its authorship and design. The general introduction serves to introduce the prophecy as that given of the Father to the Son for this present moment. It is the Word of God for this age. It is affixed with the divine seal and footnoted with a promise. The epistolary introduction is that of the Lord Jesus Christ and the Holy Spirit, the authors of the letters to the churches, whose words are to be conveyed by the human instrument, the apostle. Therefore, the epistolary introduction sets its attention upon the Lord, who is the true author of these epistles.

In the epistolary introduction, the reader is introduced to the Lord Jesus Christ in a way that is applicable to the design of the whole book. The book's purpose is to encourage and strengthen the reader in faith and confidence in the Lord. Therefore, Christ the Lord is introduced in a way that speaks to that purpose. He is called *the faithful witness*, showing Himself trustworthy and true. He is termed the *first begotten of the dead*, by which our hope is found. He lives, He reigns, and we in Him; as He has arisen from the dead and ascended on high, so we shall reign in Him. He is deemed the *prince of the kings of the earth*, which is central to our confidence and hope in the present evil age, knowing that He sovereignly governs and administers all things from above here below. When John writes, "unto him that loved us, and washed us from our sins in his own blood," he identifies the Lord as the Lamb of God, granting us great hope and joy. He also directs our attention to His blood, by which He overcame the world. When he says, "He hath made us kings and priests unto God and his Father," he raises us up to a position of certainty so that we might endure the trials of this present age with Him above. Each of these phrases are employed for our confidence, designed for our consolation, and prefatory to the revelations of Him to follow.

This grand introduction to the letters that follow prepare us for the exemplary character of these epistles. They are from the hand of our sovereign, ruling, almighty King, who is the Lamb that has prevailed, who reigns in glory, as it says, "To him be glory and dominion for ever and ever. Amen." They are also messages for our hope amidst the world's terror, as he says, "Behold, he cometh with clouds; and every eye shall see him, and they also which pierced him: and all kindreds of the earth shall wail because of him. Even so, Amen." These are pregnant epistles, filled with a grand prophetic, uniquely remarkable, and awe-inspiring form, set in an eschatological context, poised and immediate, giving the reader not only confidence, certainty, and hope, but an expectation of the urgency of this age. As if that were not enough, Christ appendixes this introduction with this affirmation, "I am Alpha and Omega, the beginning and the ending, saith the Lord, which is, and which was, and which is to come, the Almighty," making this prophecy not only urgent but certain. Perhaps no other epistle or prophecy has had so grand and awe-inspiring an introduction. This prophecy is remarkable in this way.

The third introduction found in this first chapter is a personal, apostolic introduction. It is provided by the apostle John himself. When John writes, "I John, who also am your brother, and companion in tribulation, and in the kingdom and patience of Jesus Christ, was in the isle that is called Patmos, for the word of God, and for the testimony of Jesus Christ," he sets himself with us in similar circumstance, in order to embolden us in so troubling a day. He calls himself our *companion in tribulation* so that we might see ourselves much like him. Throughout this age, the church has suffered persecution. We are assailed in this hostile world. But like John, we while in it are not of it, as he says, he was *in the kingdom and patience of Jesus Christ.* Ours is the kingdom. His is the kingdom. And afforded us in this age of tribulation is patience. John, like us, can testify to his plight but knows the joy that is set before us in Christ our Lord.

So the book of Revelation is comprised at the start with several introductions, making it unique in this way. It maintains a multifaceted authorship. There is first God the Father who has entrusted this knowledge to the Son. There is also the Spirit that is the one that makes this known, testifying to us of that which is read and heard. Last, there is John, the last living apostle, kept for this purpose, to finish God's word and to complete the book and see that it is delivered to the elect. Together, these all unite to prepare that given to complete the glorious work of the Lord started so long ago.

We find that John's introduction includes the setting of the book; it was written during John's short exile in Patmos, off the coast of Ephesus, where he had made residence ever since Rome's destruction of Jerusalem in AD 70. John indicates the reason for his exile, saying, "It was for the word of God, and the testimony of Jesus Christ," which allows him to find common ground with the reader as one suffering persecution. Given in the year AD 96, Revelation is a fitting capstone on the special revelation of God, given to His Son, for His people, until the end of all things. John's days were nearly done. A final task was his to complete. So that we might find consolation, he suffered and was persecuted by Rome. So that he might complete the work the Lord ordained him for he did not perish in the oil of his torture. So that we might know these things he was called to which he saw. So with his remaining strength, John, the apostle whom Jesus loved, who once heard Jesus say to Peter of himself, "If I will that he tarry till I come, what is that to thee" (John 21:22), takes up to write that final word of the Lord and complete the full canon of scripture.

The apostle further adds the situation leading to his first *revelation*, it was the *Lord's Day*, that day set apart from the Sabbath of the Jews, which the church was granted for the worship and delight in the Lord. What a fitting day to begin the last epistles of our Lord to His church. It is on that day that John's attention is arrested by a trumpet, a sounding blare, which draws His attention to a glorious and preemptory scene; Christ is seen in all His glory. He that once walked with the apostle, He whose breast John laid upon on the night of His betrayal, He that was last seen ascending on the mount, days before Pentecost, is now seen alive, above, glorified, enthroned, and reigning on high. Christ introduces Himself as the *Alpha and the Omega*, indicating to the reader the purpose of the book; it is to sum up all things. It is to show that He is the sum of all things. It is to show that He is sovereign, alive, active, and working, to bring an end to all the furious chaos and trouble below. It is at this point that Christ directs the apostle to pen the proceeding epistle to the seven churches. John, turning to see the Lord, observes Him in all His splendor. What he sees provides two insights: one, that Christ is glorified and active in this present day, and two, that a precedent is established for the interpretation of what is seen; what John sees is subsequently explained. Like the parables of Christ, this revelation is to be understood, and the understanding is to come from the information provided.

What John sees is a view of Christ that is intentional and representative. He is shown Christ in a way that provides insight into His work and person. It is not that He is glorious just for the sake of glory, but every aspect of what John does see is metaphorical and illustrative of the revelation provided. What John sees is useful. What John sees is applicable. What John sees is necessary for the message conveyed in the book. Whatever John saw, whatever he endeavored to explain, it was all designed to be of use. Many of the images John sees are as dreams, illusions, wonders beheld, which are pictures of truths conveyed. It is here that Christ establishes the book's hermeneutic, in saying that the stars in His hand and the candlesticks around which He walks are but symbols of what they represent. He provides a clear understanding that they are word pictures given to convey meaning. Any attempt therefore to literalize the images of the book defies the very construct of the book's design. Just as Jesus never was a door, or a lamb, or a loaf of bread, so He is not carrying in His hand *stars*; as He says, the stars are but the messengers of the churches. They are in

His right hand because they are in His control, under His dominion, and directed by His authority. John may have not physically seen what he explains, it was a vision, and it was merely a vision provided for our instruction and understanding of that which the images were designed to convey.

Therefore, understand that every detail of Christ's appearance adds insight into His nature and person. The white hair implies His wisdom and eternal nature as well as His impeccability and purity. His brass feet show that He has been tried by fire. He has endured persecution and trial. His fiery eyes show He pierces the hearts of men with knowledge, that He is omniscient, omnipresent, and immense. The thunder of His voice indicates His majesty and glory. How He appears bears the image of the High Priest so that we see the setting in a familiar context. He is active, working, interceding, directing, He is our Mediator and King. He is, amidst the candlesticks, His church, which He serves day and night. Christ never had a sword protruding from His mouth, but His words are the eternal Logos, the Word of God, which is as a two-edged sword. The vision given John is like all those in the book; they begin in the temple of heaven, Christ the Mediator, King, and High Priest, doing the will of the Father, by way of the Spirit, unto the end God has foreordained. Every vision proceeds from above, the throne of God, His glory, unto the end He has determined. While the candlesticks are seven, though in the temple there was one, it is seven for two reasons; one, there are seven literal churches to whom the letter was sent, and second, they represent the universal church of Christ, throughout this age, in circumstance and situation. The number 7 throughout this book is a recurring number representing a whole, as creation was a week of seven, so is the work of God and that representing His in the count of seven.

John's response to Christ in all His glory is but indicative of the way in which Christ is glorified and magnified in this book. Christ is shown this way in order to strengthen a feeble church, to encourage the persecuted bride, to grant faith and patience to His own in the scope of an age fueled with rage, fury, warfare, and wrath, so that we might know that above is certainty, confidence, and might while below is trouble. This is the book of a sovereign, eternal, almighty

Lamb, who reigns above, working actively in accordance with the divine will, to complete, to sum up, to conclude in this age his work and the eternal will of God. Christ's words to John, "Fear not, I am the first and the last," tell us that we are to be encouraged and comforted in this book. He says, "I am alive forevermore," reminding us, and the apostle that He has not left nor forsaken us; He reigns alive. When He says, "I have the keys of hell and of death," He reminds us that He is the one that sovereignly unlocks the mystery of time and this present age, working to conclude that with which He has been entrusted, our salvation, the world's judgment, and the Father's glory forever and ever, amen.

CHAPTER 2 AND 3 OVERVIEW

Chapters 2 and 3 of Revelation are to be taken as a whole; they are that which Christ said, are *the things which are*; the things *which were* are those images of chapter 1. The images of chapter 1 will carry into the next two and be applied accordingly. These next two chapters comprise the seven letters of Christ to the seven churches of Asia Minor at the end of the apostolic age. John knew these churches well, having been in Ephesus for nearly thirty years, AD 70–98. An abundance of early church testimony places John in Ephesus before and after His exile to Patmos. F. F. Bruce notes, "Clement of Alexandria, for example, says that after Domitian's death (AD 96) 'John the apostle' moved from the island of Patmos to Ephesus-a statement which may go back to Hegesippus."[1] They were the churches of his immediate oversight. Ephesus was where John spent his last thirty years of life; it was that central church of Asia Minor started by the apostle Paul, which had been raised out of the ashes of the world's idolatry. It was the church Timothy was sent to so that he might put things in order. It was there that John took up residence once Rome destroyed Jerusalem for one final time, clearing away the relics of a past age, in accordance with the sovereign design of the Lord. First and foremost, chapters 2 and 3 are a snapshot of the church at the height of Roman persecution and the end of an era.

The seven letters contain Christ's instructions, reproofs, encouragements, and warnings to the seven churches. They are the churches

---

[1] St. John at Ephesus. F. F. BRUCE, MA, BA. Rylands professor of Biblical Criticism and Exegesis in the University of Manchester.

of Pergamum, Thyatira, Philadelphia, Smyrna, Sardis, Laodicea, and Ephesus. These churches were immersed in trial, suffering persecution; they were being inundated with heresy, overrun by worldliness, they had been long in suffering and waiting the Lord's return, they were churches, of which some dead, others dying, and some callous and indifferent to their King. These words are those *things that are*, which the Lord said He would reveal to the apostle, in order to affirm the present state of things. The church appeared in peril. These chapters were oh so needed to shore up their confidence and set them back on the proper course. Like all other New Testament epistles, these two chapters address the church's faith, troubles, and needs in this world. They hear from the voice of He that sits enthroned above, and like all epistles, these truths have lasting bearing upon the church throughout this age. We may therefore say that these two chapters are at once pertinent to the day in which they were written, but also imperative to the church throughout these last days.

Chapters 2 and 3 Analysis

What is here is telling. We find seven churches that are in various states of turmoil. Four are in disarray, one is pressed, and two are in peril. Together, they all have three common traits they share. For many, there is first the issue of the heart. For most, there is the threat of heresy. Many are exhausted and spent. Some have given way to callous death. Overall, each church is in a perilous state and desperately needs to hear from the throne of heaven. Thus, with John the last apostle soon to be fetched away forever, and Rome's lust for Christian blood on the rise, a dispatch from the King was vital. Revelation 2 and 3 are foremost directives of the King above to His own below. His words are urgent; they are designed so that they might embolden His own to hold fast and not lose heart, and most of all, they are intended to instruct the churches as to the reasons for their current predicament. Each of the seven churches were in a perilous state, and in fact, those of the church throughout this age have found themselves equally in a perilous condition, in need of such council. For here below, things most often appear perilous, if not lost.

What is omitted in these two chapters is also telling. Christ's address to the churches omits much of what churches have disputed over for centuries. The Lamb of God does not address form and practice, which undoubtedly present by this point in early church history, does not at that point in time exist in full. Still, not a word is said. Christ does not speak about baptisms and ceremonies. He does not allude to traditions and form; rather, He addresses matters more essential to the faith itself. He addresses doctrine and faith. His attention and care for the churches is telling. Christ is concerned for the heart. The affections of the churches lie central to Christ's instructions. Those that have grown cold, indifferent, and careless in godly affections are warned and threatened while those that are persevering and laboring in Christian charity are comforted and encouraged. Error is denounced, heresy repulsed, and apostacy judged; but trivial matters are left untouched, teaching us that the truth of the gospel is foremost in Christ's attention and the affections of the heart are of His utmost concern.

Much exposition of these chapters exists to date. There is not much in question regarding their content. These were actual churches, they existed in the western region of Asia Minor. The circumstances addressed were historical. All this is true. There were errors in these churches of which history has only scant evidence. Heresies were already in play, from the Nicolaitans to those called the synagogue of Satan, there is little surprise to find that false teaching was rampant. And while the former error appears to address a form of first-century Gnosticism and the latter a Jewish error, our Lord's attention here is not so much to the identify of these errors as it is to the care of those under duress. Christ's attention is to the state of these churches; they were in peril. The church in the waning days of the apostolic age were under duress; they were in a hostile, idolatrous Roman world, they had remnants of the Judaizers that were foremost troublers of the early church remaining, they were living in a time of great tribulation, and that tribulation was to endure for yet a time. It is this trouble that our Lord addresses.

Understanding the content of each of the seven short epistles involves identifying the pattern found in each short epistle. First, the letters are divided into four principal parts. They have the introduction of the Lord Himself, they have the identity of the church they address, they then possess an analysis of the state of the particular church in question, and they have a final admonition of the Lord to the church. If the church in question has concerns, they are addressed. If they are in danger, they are warned. If they are in peril, they are admonished. If they are negligent in their faith, they are cautioned. If they are complacent or complicit in error or in the truth, they are adjured. But as any other New Testament epistle, they are each and every one an epistle.

Where they stand alone is that the letters are couched in metaphor and symbol. Each of the symbols were purposely introduced in the first chapter. Thus, when the Lord is introduced to each church, He is introduced in accordance with His introduction in 1:12–20 in chapter 1. *The things which were* therefore are used to explain *the things which are*; in other words, Jesus was introduced the way He was introduced in chapter 1 for the very purpose of using that image to address each church in the following two chapters. The Lord is seen in each letter as He was in chapter 1, the difference being that the aspects of His appearance are employed specifically to the application given to each church. For example, to Smyrna, Jesus is seen as He was in chapter 1 as the "First and the Last, which was dead, and is now alive," a fitting image for those enduring trial, who shall yet endure another time of tribulation for yet *ten days*. So understand that each depiction of Christ is purposed for the church addressed, for their situations and needs, so that they might be emboldened in Christ. Comprehending the content of each letter begins with understanding how Christ is introduced back in chapter 1.

In chapter 1, we saw Christ with a head of white; this speaks to His divine wisdom and age. He is from everlasting; He is working all things according to His eternal purpose. He is the first and the last, the Alpha and the Omega, whose wisdom and knowledge are unsearchable. The sword protruding from His mouth is not only His sovereign, eternal word, but also that by which He makes war and conquers His foes. His brass feet speak to His having been tried and having prevailed. His long garment speaks to His holiness and majesty. His eyes of flaming fire speak to His omniscience and omnipotence. His thundering voice speaks of His divine majesty as God. Altogether, the reason John saw Jesus as He did in chapter 1 was to employ that image to the good and use of each church thereafter. In all, we see Jesus gloried in His eternal attributes and from them we, like the seven churches, derive strength to persevere and to endure until the end. The central theme of our Lord's sovereignty over all creation and this age is bound up in His appearance in chapter 1, used purposedly to the design of each church in the chapters following. His titles, His place, His actions, and His appearance, each are purposed to embolden the church in this present age.

Ephesus needed to see the Lord in heaven standing amidst His churches, laboring, working. As the central hub of apostolic labors, Ephesus had a particular primacy of importance in first century ecclesiastical affairs. Smyrna, which I have already addressed, was greatly engaged in tribulation, this church needed the image of Christ as He *which was dead, and is alive*. Pergamum needed the image of the sword, as in her midst was Satan's seat and the sword was needed for battle against those foes. Thyatira needed the piercing eyes of the omniscient One, who could see and discern those who were faithful and those who were not. Sardis needed the threat of expulsion, by Him who holds the stars in His hand, whose seven Spirits are discerning, by Him that possesses the means of life, since Sardis was as dead. Philadelphia needed the key of David, the covenant promise made to the true seed of Abraham, to refute those calling themselves Jews, a kingdom that the Lord alone opens to those of His divine, sovereign call. While Laodicea needed to hear from Him that is *faithful and true*, whose words will not fail, who threatens those that are unfaithful and callous toward Him. Each image to each church was purposed and properly applied.

Once introduced, the heart of each epistle addressed the state of each church. The situation in Ephesus involved a church with a heart afflicted with fading love; they were a church that in her first generation embraced their beloved Paul, who in her passing days needed Timothy to set things in order and, in her third generation, had the apostle of love himself in their midst but still found their love growing cold. This is a reminder to us all that often they who have been so blessed for so long often finds such blessings taken for granted. Ephesus had fought the good fight. They had expelled the false apostles. They hated the Nicolaitans. Yet despite all their labors and perseverance, their hearts were growing cold. It is not surprising to find Ephesus in the state of waning affections, for far too often, those engaged in the battle find their hearts growing callous over time. Such is the case throughout the history of the church in this and the previous age, which tends toward cooling affections. When the church is found in this condition, it is a perilous one. For lively affections are vital to the life of the church. Reminding Ephesus that they are to persevere until the end in love, our Lord sets the image of the tree of life before them, as it is kept for those that endure until the end. He who is the author and finisher of our faith adjures them to press on until the end.

In Smyrna, the faithful, bloodied church, there the Lord appeared to encourage and embolden His faithful ones. They had already endured much at the hands of the Jews. So like a gentle Shepherd and merciful King, He stoops to give them a sip of the water of life so that they might rise up once more and press forth in the battle, knowing that while it will be for yet another space of time, ten days, it shall be for only a short time, yet ten days. So as most time indicators in Revelation are defined by their purpose, so here the ten days speak to the determined yet short time of their coming trial. Ramsey says, "The promise implies that these persecutions shall continue, and shall be suffered to run their complete natural course, indicated here, after the manner of this book, by ten days, expressing a complete but definite period" (Ramsey, 137). This small church, standing in the shadows of mighty Ephesus, who were faithful and steadfast in their love for Christ, serve as a lesson to us all throughout the age. It is a reminder for us to not consider ourselves too minor or insignificant in the sight of our Savior, for He promises to us as He did to Smyrna, "I will give thee a crown of life."

In Pergamum, the dangers were real. Idolatry was rampant, and friendship with the world was a mortal threat. Thus, the sword was necessary, necessary to separate truth from error, necessary to divide asunder and discern those true; it was necessary to slay those of the seat of Satan. They had endured. They had held fast in the days of trial. So much so that the name of Antipas the faithful martyr remains. Pergamum was a city of wealth, one of great renown, yet also a city of worldliness, as Ramsey wrote, "Pergamos…had once been the capital for a century and a half of a wealthy kingdom, and which still was renowned for its magnificence, riches, and the treasures of learning stored in its vast library." This was a city of the world and the church in it was seen sojourning in the seat of Satan. Two errors were rampant in Pergamum: first, the error of Balaam, and second, the error of the Nicolaitans. The first involved unholy alliances with the world, and the latter, false doctrine. Both were deadly. See how Christ threatens to make war with the word of His mouth. The Word of God alone is our sword. See how He addresses His own directly through the Spirit. See how He promises those things that shall throughout the book be promised to those that overcome. Hidden manna is the covenant bread of life. The white stone is Christ our cornerstone. The new name is Christian, beloved, His bride, she who overcomes. A message to the church throughout this age to keep pure in the truth and to have no alliances with this world.

In Thyatira, false doctrine and heretical teachers were threatening her life. Heresy is always leaven, and it threatens to leaven the whole lump. It is that idolatry that Jezebel brought to Ahab and the apostate kingdom of Israel. It is comingling the world's idols with Christ. Oddly, Thyatira had much to be commended for in the way of mercy and kindness, which, as it were, may have been the means by which the serpent found a pathway to slither into her midst. She was commended for her latter works but warned by her tolerance. So often, it is the case that good intentions are used to poison the whole lot. The church of Thyatira was like the ecumenical and social gospel movements of our day, which for the sake of peace will compromise truth and exchange purity with error, all for the sake of peace. It was Jezebel that brought idols of Tyre into Israel by way of marriage, and it were those in Thyatira who had brought the idols of the day into the church. Heresy cannot be tolerated. It is a poison that slays. It is that which leads many down the path of fornication with the world for the sake of ecumenic peace and ultimately death and a darkness like the setting sun. Thus is Christ presented as the morning star that shall arise in their midst as truth and light.

In Sardis, a shell remained, a lifeless church, she was a church that had the outward form of a church, but not the inner light of life. Sardis was dead. It is indicative of the visible church that remains when the true church is extinct. Sardis was a city of pomp and wealth, perhaps the most beautiful of all Asia, which today is but a wasteland. When and how it came alive is uncertain, but by the time of John's last days, it was obsolete. It was a corpse. While a few remained that were the Lord's, the visible church itself was but a cold, callous graveyard, filled with those that Christ has nothing good or bad to address. There are no words of specific concern, no hated things, no cherished things, but only this, Sardis had a reputation for her works. To the world the church of Sardis lived, but to the Lord, she was dead. How often the church in history has had such a reputation, as though alive to the world but dead to the Lord. His analysis is abrupt. His words callous. His directions cold. She is to know Him as a thief shortly. Yet those that endure until the end shall know Him as faithful and true, for their names are written in the book of life.

Philadelphia, like Smyrna, escapes censure. She is faithful. She is beloved. Though weak, she is still strong. She has fought the fight of faith against legalists and naysayers. She is in need of His strength. History has often seen the vestiges of the seemingly feeble church, which to the world is not strong, but in Christ shall overcome. Christ speaks to her gently, speaking of keeping her from further tribulation, even that which is sure to come. How amazing that she stood in the shadows of churches like Ephesus and Sardis, yet she had persevered while they had not. It is Philadelphia that is promised to be a pillar in the temple of the Lord and to bear the name of our Lord and His city forever. Such words were not only a great encouragement to the feeble church of Philadelphia, but also to those throughout this age that have been feeble but beloved. The Lord our God shall keep us and bring us safely through.

Last, there was the church of Laodicea, a church of the world, wealthy, going about their religion with callous indifference. To them, Christ's words were an annoyance, a trifling, something to be ignored. They did not need Him. They had all things necessary in this world. They are the church that was plagued with a serpent's bite but knew themselves not in peril. Christ was right before them as the bronze staff before Israel in the wilderness, but they had no desire to look up and live. The church of Laodicea had no need of the Lord. They bartered in the world's wares and were content to be without heavenly goods. How sad that any church could ever exist that has no need of Christ. Yet such is often the case in the history of the church, where she seems more irritated to think of Christ than joyful to hear His name. So Christ stands above Laodicea as the "amen," the faithful and true, the beginning of the creation of God, the sovereign Lord and judge that shall call all to account that spurn Him. Laodicea, a church bitten to death, but dull to her wound. She whom the Lord was most incensed toward of all.

In total, the seven churches of Asia Minor were all in distinct and separate conditions. They all lived in the same world. They all were sister cities. Yet each had their own predicaments and trials. Some were greatly applauded of by the world. Some were wealthy in the world. Others were weak and frail, feeble and forlorn. Still, overall, they all were under the care of Christ. It was He that governed their world and their lives. It was He that was the High Priest of their confession. He sovereignly was administering their condition in that day, just as He does today. And while each of these churches remain as an echo to us all, an echo of the seven abiding conditions of the church throughout this age, they still were the churches of their day. When John stood upon the shores of Patmos hearing the Great I Am speak to the churches of His oversight, surely he could not help but remember them and their plight. The apostle had once walked their streets and observed their ways. Now he was their messenger. And unto us throughout this age the apostle equally writes. Revelation 2 and 3 serve as a lasting warning and discerning test to the church in every age, echoed by the words of our Lord who says, "He who has an ear let him hear." From the things which were to the things which are, now comes those things *which shall shortly come to pass.*

CHAPTERS 4–22
INTRODUCED

The fourth chapter of Revelation begins the portion of the book Christ before identified as "the things which shall shortly come to pass." These are the things following the apostolic age, the things of this present age, those revelations of God's work in these last days, these called the latter days, spanning from the apostolic era to the final coming of Christ. Simply put, the majority of the book of Revelation covers from the year AD 96 until the return of Christ. The previous age of history was from approximately 4100 BC and lasted until AD 30; it began with creation and ended with Pentecost. That age along with this present age are the only two ages biblically defined, summing up the whole of time. So there were the days before Christ, and there are the days since Christ. History is simply made up of these two ages. Biblically, the Old Testament through the Gospels cover the last age while the rest of the New Testament covers this age. Acts spans from Christ's ascension in AD 30 to the mid- to late AD 60s. The Pauline epistles and James coincide with the time period of Acts. The general epistles beyond James are all post AD 60. This leaves Revelation, the last of the epistles, and the only New Testament prophetic book, which spans from AD 96, when John was in Patmos, to the end of this age. Revelation 2–3 is the epistolary portion of the book; it is applicable to the late first-century AD. The rest of Revelation, chapters 4–22, covers from the close of the first century to Christ's return. This is that Christ spoke of as "the things which shall shortly come to pass."

The rest of Revelation then, that time identified by our Lord as *the things which shall shortly come to pass*, consists of those things that transpire during this age from start to finish. This post-apostolic age is thematically divided in Revelation into three parts; the three parts consist of that first that is sealed within a scroll that has been sealed with seven seals, that next which is ushered in by the sounding of seven trumpets, and that finally which is contained within seven bowls. Together, these three sections comprise the eternal design of God to consummate our salvation and the world's judgment in this the last days.

We find that the seals demonstrate the eternal design and plan of God, His will for this age. The trumpets announce the active work of God's providence to sovereignly conquer the nations of this world through this age. Here He advances His kingdom through the events that befall the world in this age. With the bowls, the judgment of God, the pouring out of His wrath exemplifies the war between the Lord upon His throne and Satan and his allies below. In all, these three parts make up this third portion of the book, which is a grand overview of the things brought to pass in this the last age. We could sum up this age as the age of Christ's reign and conquest, whereby He goes forth to conquer, to execute the fierceness of the wrath of the Almighty, in accordance with the foreordained will of God. All things that come to pass in this age are designed of God, they proceed from heaven and the throne of the reigning Lord, and this is the age of the culmination of the Lord's just redemptive glory, planned from before the foundations of the world.

We find then that chapters 4–8:1 are the first of three perspectival views of God's work in this age. The first is from the perspective of the foreordination of God, the view of the Lord's eternal decrees for this age. Chapters 8:2–11 contain the second view, whereby we are given a perspective of our Lord's governance in this world throughout this present age. Chapters 12–22 are the final view, wherein we observe the culmination of the execution of God's judgment and salvation to the end of this age. Each of these three visions are set in the construct of seven. Seven is likened unto a creation week, and just as God created the world in six days and on the seventh, He rested, so are these three views of God's divine work set in a parallel form of seven to highlight the divine glory of God in this age. These three parts form a grand synopsis of God's purpose all along, showing what He has planned from the beginning. Our Lord is central to that plan. Christ is sent forth to conquer sin and death and to subdue all nations. He is sent to execute judgment and the fierceness of the Lord. He is sent to finish the work of salvation and redemption. In Him and by His reign, we find the compendium of God's glory; it is a synopsis of God's eternal plan to be finalized in these last days. Overall, Revelation 4–22 contains a lofty view of the history of the end of the world.

As has been mentioned, each of the three perspectives in Revelation 4–22 is introduced as proceeding from the throne of God. The first vision is the longest of them all, this view of the heavenly throne sets down the glory and majesty of our Lord on high for all that follows. For the reader, it is encouraging, it is comforting to him amidst the turmoil in this world, and it is emboldening to all saints to know that what is seen below is fully under the governance and oversight of an active and all powerful, just sovereign above. He, who despite appearances, reigns victorious and is seen conquering and certain to complete that conquest in the end. He shall do so, for He reigns above, far above the chaos below. Below, there is violence and persecution; above, there is calm. Below, sorrow and grief; above, certainty and holy majesty. All doubts that those of John's day might have had due to the great tribulation and persecution they suffered at the hands of the Romans certainly would be quelled by what John is shown above. Shall it not have that effect upon all throughout the chaos and clamor of this age? What is more comforting than our God reigning on high? What is more encouraging than knowing that all things work together for good to those of us loved of God? What is more emboldening than knowing that the schemes of those of this world are used to their own judgment while we are kept in Christ above? This book is so very important to the church of this present age, as it contains that blessed confidence necessary to stand amidst the fray.

Chapter 4–8:1 Overview

The first section of that which is to take place *shortly after these things* is a synopsis of the divine foreordained plan for this age. It begins with a sealed scroll and ends with its contents revealed. It is a scroll that is written in eternity past, sealed, and kept until this age, during which it is now to be revealed. It is a scroll containing all that God has willed and designed for these last days. It is written within and without, with nowhere left to write, as nothing is to be added or removed from it, for it is complete and has been that way since before time began. Remember, this book is figurative, symbolic, seen through visions and dreams, so what John is seeing is merely that which represents the mind of God revealed.

But now, Christ has prevailed, and having completed all that was determined in the past age, now is prepared that which has been decreed for this age. So our Lord rises from the throne to take that scroll from He that is veiled and hidden in holiness, and open it, so that it might be made known what is to be accomplished in this age. He is to bring to pass all that was determined for this age unto the end of time. So our Lord steps forth to take and direct the things contained within the scroll. He is to direct this age from His throne. Contained within the book are the designs of God in the world throughout this age, all things, be they warfare, famine, plight, or plague, all are designed of the Lord and in accordance with His perfect plan. The contents themselves being subordinate to Christ's ultimate purpose, to subdue all foes and complete this age by delivering up His own unto final salvation and eternal life.

And just as God purposed to create a world in six days before time began and usher in a glorious rest and reflection upon His perfect design, so He has purposed in this age to complete that which was begun, to do so in the likeness of those days, and usher in a final rest. The pattern of sevens in this portion of Revelation has that design. The Lord will complete His work in this age in the scope of seven, in the likeness of creation's days, and it will be very good. In the end, a final sabbath rest shall come. In the end, He will complete all He has foreordained. He will do so from His throne, as the Son of God has prevailed to conduct this age until its determined end. For the reader, no greater confidence and comfort can be found to know that "all things work together for good to those loved of God," knowing that our Lord rules over heaven and earth, and that our God is dictating all things that come to pass. This first of revelations found within the likeness of a scroll is for this last age and it contains the details for us of all that is to come and to rest knowing that all that comes to pass is of the Lord. It is right, it is good, and it is necessary, for it is of God. As heaven opens up to John, all the turmoil and trial of life below fades away; for above, all is well, while below, the Lord brings to pass all He has ordained.

CHAPTER 4 AND 5 ANALYSIS

A HEAVENLY PERSPECTIVE

Chapters 4 and 5 are to be taken as a whole, as they contain those prefatory events necessary to the completion of the will of God found in the several chapters that follow. As all things that transpire in time come from the throne of the Almighty, it is necessary that the story begin at His throne. In the previous chapters, John was shown *the things which were* (Christ attending to His church) and *the things which are* (the state of the Asian church), all from the shores of Patmos while he was in the Spirit on the Lord's Day. As he is now to be shown the things shortly to come to pass hereafter, his vantage point must change. All that is at hand comes first from above, from there it is to be observed. So it is as if a door to heaven was opened to give John the vantage point necessary for that which was to follow. Thus, we read, "After this I looked, and, behold, a door was opened in heaven: and the first voice which I heard was as it were of a trumpet talking with me; which said, Come up hither, and I will shew thee things which must be hereafter."

We must recall that this is but a prophecy, a vision to be shown; there is no actual door, the door to heaven merely represents the change of perspective necessary for the apostle to observe the revelation to follow. Further, when John says, "immediately I was in the spirit," we understand the apostle is not translated to heaven bodily. Nothing in prophetic language or form allows for any other interpretation of these words; all that happens is that John, who is on the island of Patmos at the end of the first-century AD is now given a vision of that which is shortly to come to pass from the perspective of heaven above. He is to see in a vision that heaven is dictating all that occurs on the Earth below. It does not appear that we are to understand that he was bodily translated to heaven, neither should we imagine that this passage is an allusion to some other event or *rapture*; simply put, heaven was opened to John, and he was *in the spirit* to see that which was emblematic of things to come.

The first thing John sees is the inner sanctum of our sovereign God. The point has been made; all things begin at the throne of God. What John begins to see is indicative of the fact that what comes to pass in this age, as the last of ages, is all that God has foreordained. What a glorious thought! Nothing that transpires in heaven or earth is but what God wills. Revelation 4 begins with John being shown the throne of God and from that throne this comfort, that He has a plan for this age. The Lord has determined this age before it ever comes to pass. When John sees heaven, it is not a cloud God is seen sitting upon, instead He is seen upon a throne. God rules from a throne. He is a sovereign that governs and rules all things. He sits in judgment and reigns over this world and all things in heaven and in earth. Nothing is beyond His plan or oversight, all things are of Him, to Him, and through Him, and it is His to see that all things are completed. He is high above all the chaos of earth below, working His perfect will. Here is the perfect reminder to John and the reader that God remains seated on His throne above, nothing has unseated Him; He remains ruler of heaven and earth. All things proceed from His throne and those things He has foreordained.

Remarkably, while the throne of God is seen, the Father remains veiled in obscurity. John likens the One that sits on the throne to precious stones, and these stones are indicative of His person, but His person is not seen. All that is seen are those facets of His glory contained with His nature; John sees His divine attributes. Remember that everything represents something, so what John sees of the Father are but the radiations of His glory. With finite, human words he strains to describe what he sees. He sees the reflections of the Almighty, and he likens those reflections to facets of gems. What else could John use to describe the One that is indescribable? How can you explain an incorporeal, incomprehensible, immense, and perfect being, but with the most precious of earthly stones? Nothing on earth can compare; His glory is beyond human words. The chaos and trouble John just left below in a moment is calmed by the scene above.

As John seeks to describe what he sees, he looks to that on earth that is spectacular. He considers the likeness of God to a jasper and sardine stone. These two stones alone are all John speaks of; it is what he sees of the reflection of Him that sits upon the throne. John merely sees the effulgence of His glory. He sees the reflections of the divine being, but even they are veiled in glory. James Ramsey says, "Jasper, is an appropriate symbol of the variety of infinite and lovely excellencies that blend together in the character of God; and the blood red of the sardine or cornelian is an equally appropriate symbol of that justice that pervades, and is inseparably united with, all His other attributes" (p. 229). What is seen is merely reflective of His glory; we do not see Him. With comforting words John describes that emanated from the throne of God as reflections of His glory and person. He is seen as majestic and regal, eternal and omnipotent.

Even more, the throne is overshadowed by a rainbow, immediately provoking thoughts of His eternal covenant, which is ever above His throne. Ezekiel saw it, "I saw as it were the appearance of fire, and it had brightness round about. As the appearance of the bow that is in the cloud in the day of rain, so was the appearance of the brightness round about" (Ezek. 1:27f). Now John sees it. It is likened unto an emerald, which Ramsey calls, "The well understood emblem of peace" (p. 229). It is seen as a reminder to all that God's covenant promise of redemption for this accursed world is not forgotten; the sign and seal of His covenant promise is always set above Him as a blessed reminder to all. But that is all. We see nothing more of Him who is veiled in splendor. He remains too glorious to behold. But what we see is what is necessary; we see that He is divine and glorious, seated on the throne above all, and bearing the reminder of the covenant of His grace. Then, from that throne and effulgence of His glory comes forth an arm, and not just any arm, but His right arm, which is an ever-present reminder of His strength and majesty. The arm extends to produce a scroll, a scroll written upon and sealed. He has kept it. It is His alone. It contains all that He has designed for time itself. It is an emblem of His eternal will. The King has written His decrees; it is an ancient scroll, as it was written and sealed long ago by the ancient of days.

Let us remember that chapter 4 is the beginning of the first of three divisions in Revelation; this begins that which Christ called the things that are to *shortly come to pass.* These three divisions will cover the scope of God's sovereign grace and providence in this present age. All three sections begin from the throne of God, so this first of visions will span the texts of chapters 4 to chapter 8 verse 1; this is the vision of God's eternal decrees for this present age. All that we shall see in these chapters will detail the eternal plan of God, written and sealed from before the foundations of the world. The events of the fourth chapter begin that process necessary to the completion of the foreordained plan of God. The Son, having prevailed, is now able to rise and take that which has been kept for this very moment. Here is that which has long been anticipated; Christ is to take the scroll and undertake that which was written long ago.

As the seals are loosed, we will observe that everything in this age, from Christ's enthronement to His return are all planned of God, they are foreordained from before time, purposed and prepared. As it was in the previous age, so it is in this age. The Lord has written the events of time. Everything that occurs in every age is of His design. This kingdom age is no different, for it has been written in the annals of God's decrees from before all things began. From the throne of God, the vision begins and from His throne comes to pass all He has decreed; from the Father to the Son, the scroll of His divine foreordained will is to be conveyed and revealed as the Son will execute that plan. He will dispatch the necessary forces to accomplish those eternal decrees. They are complete, forever inscribed, filling the scroll front and back, immutable, certain, and they shall come to pass. Chapters 4 and 5, which are prefatory to the revelation of the divine eternal plan that Christ the Lord shall unseal, show us that the

Lord sovereignly rules and governs this age, just as He has the past. All things are foreordained of God.

But let us not pass by this scene too quickly. The rainbow above the throne of God reminds us that He is a covenant God, He who not only makes but keeps His promises. A central tenant of the prophecy is to impress upon the reader that our sovereign God has a purpose in all things. He is not merely sovereign. He is covenantally sovereign. He plans to save. He will keep His promises. Revelation is written in order to bolster our courage and our courage rests alone upon the promises of our God. The promises of God are that upon which we endure this troublesome life. The things shown in this book are unsettling, often terrifying, and certainly threatening, but what better to buttress the saints of the living Lamb than the covenant reminder of our God. It is His covenant that testifies of His love for us eternally. As John beholds the rainbow round about the throne of God, he reminds us of God's covenant of redemption. The rainbow serves to reminds us of His will to save. It assures us of His justice sure to be executed. But also, of His mercy. When we see the rainbow, we remember the everlasting mercy of our God.

Shall we forget? We are *chosen in Him from before the foundations of the world.* Our eternal election is built upon His faithful promises; without them, where would be our hope? In ourselves? What hope is that? For the god of man's imagination is built upon the effort and determination of men, but the biblical God is the eternal, covenanting Sovereign, who knows us, who numbers us as His own, to the exact count so that none are lost, who faithfully is bringing us to His glory and our bliss. The rainbow is the most necessary of sights, reminding us that God has an eternal covenant, a redemptive design for grace, which is a central theme of this book. Its radiance reflects His plan which shall be completed to utter perfection. As He redeems a fallen world, as He judges a vagrant and hostile cosmos, bringing justice to those arrayed against their Creator, God alone is sure to restore and reclaim that which was lost in accordance with His eternal will. The rainbow is not only a personal note to all the elect, but also a declaration to heaven and earth that the Creator of all things is sovereignly working to complete His eternal design of redemption.

We, also in these two chapters, get our first glimpse of the elect of God, His chosen, from first to last, which are here represented by the twenty-four elders, who are symbolic of the twelve sons of Israel and the twelve apostles. They remind us that God's redeemed are fully accounted for in heaven. These twenty-four elders represent the church of the last age and the church of this age. They are representatives of all Israel, Jew and Gentile, from first to last. Remember that this is a vision, nothing more. Clearly, John does not see himself, but he sees those in a vision that represent those to whom he was part. He sees the full church of the ages represented by their own appointed heads, who are chosen to serve, honor, glorify, worship, and enjoy Him forever. Flowing from the throne are those elect, chosen, redeemed, who make up a number beyond estimation, represented by a sea of glass, seen flowing from His throne. Where else would they be but before Him? Their presence testifies not only of their proximity to His heart, but also to His plan, as we are seen in these representatives crowned with His glory, victorious, and arrayed in His garments of imputed righteousness.

See how close we reside to Him. See how our place is prepared. See what wonders and glories await us above. The opening scene prepares for what follows by showing to us the calm, blessed estate of heaven, which is far from the chaos and clamor of the wicked world below. As the prophecy will show us, that great and terrifying upheaval and havoc brought below by the allied forces of the devil is futile; this vision will appease those fears by contrasting them with the serenity of the glorious habitation of our Lord. He sits enthroned. Nothing can or will dethrone Him. Nothing escapes Him. Nothing is lost to His sovereign will and glory, and best of all, all that comes to pass proceeds from that which He purposed long ago. He brings all things to pass to a good and perfect end, echoed by the thundering forth of thunder from His throne certain to terrify those below. All this is contained in this image is reminiscent of that which once stood upon the earth. The scene is foreshadowed by the earthly temple. Here above is the antitype. As the Lord's glory once filled the

Holiest, assuring Israel that none should prevail against them, so here such assurance follows.

Also found in this vision are the symbolic seven Spirits and candlesticks, 7 being the number of completeness in this prophecy. While there is but one Spirit, He is seen in the count of seven, by which He is the One who proceeds to accomplish all things according to the divine will in a full and complete sense. The seven *aspects* of the Spirit, fueling the seven *candlesticks* tended to by the Lord, shows that the church on earth is tended to in heaven above by Him that is our Great High Priest. That church is filled with His eternal Spirit. We saw Him before and will see Him again in the garb of the High Priest, which is His duty. His image is found here in the four beasts surrounding that throne. In those beasts we see Him, the full glory of Him as man, divine, servant, and king, as Ezekiel once saw. The beasts reflect that seen of Him in the gospels, of His majesty, service, humanity, and divinity. The eyes all about signifying His divine knowledge, His omniscience, by which He oversees His own. He not only sees all but tends to all. All that John sees is the godhead, the Father, Son, and Spirit, along with Israel, His beloved, all His elect, from first to last, represented by that church of the past age and her of the present, together being one.

From this comes the reminder of that Isaiah once was taught, that our Lord is holy, all His works are holy, He is far above all evil and unrighteousness, all things that are of Him and that proceed from Him are holy. As Habakkuk testified, "The Lord is in His holy temple, let all the earth be silent before Him." It is then that the attendants of heaven are seen bowing and proclaiming the truth of the message to follow that He is "worthy, O Lord, to receive glory and honour and power: for thou hast created all things, and for thy pleasure they are and were created." All things are His. As we watch the events to follow, we shall be reminded of this often; He is holy, He is divine, He is working all things after the council of His will, all things are of Him and for Him, nothing is beyond the scope of His sovereign will and providence, and He alone is glorified, He alone is just, He alone is from everlasting, who shall and is completing all things in this age and the age before as it is intended, designed, purposed, and perfectly planned. Nothing has changed since the days when Isaiah beheld His glory until now. He remains the same; all that has changed is that His sovereign, eternal plan has advanced, His Son is now fully known, the world is drawing close to her end in judgment, and the elect are nearing their full number.

So with this initial vision, John and the reader are prepared to behold the wonders of the Father's eternal will through the Son by the Spirit. They who are holy, just, certain, and perfect are working to complete that which is from eternity designed. This age, like the former, is as perfectly planned and conducted by the sovereign will and design of God, and we should take heart. For He is sovereign, holy, and mighty, and the things that come *hereafter, shortly*, are those things He has purposed, and they will be completed to perfection; from the coming of our Lord at the first until the last when He returns, this is the prophecy of this present age. Behold! The Lord is sovereign and holy, and He has ordained whatsoever comes to pass. You can almost hear Paul's words echoing through heaven at this moment,

> What shall we then say to these things? If God be for us, who can be against us? He that spared not his own Son, but delivered him up for us all, how shall he not with him also freely give us all things? Who shall lay any thing to the charge of God's elect? It is God that justifieth. Who is he that condemneth? It is Christ that died, yea rather, that is risen again, who is even at the right hand of God, who also maketh intercession for us. (Rom. 8:31f)

In all, chapters 4 and 5 are simply the precursor to the revelation of the will of God in this age; we are observing with John what is transpiring above as the age begins and proceeds. It is the Lord's will to advance His kingdom on Earth, and by doing so, He shall gain victory over the world below. From the images of these two chapters, we are shown the impeccable and majestic glory of the godhead, who is holy, perfect, just, and mighty, who sits on the throne above heaven and Earth, who is three in one, who is not divested of His creation but completely invested in it, as He has worked to the onset of this age for this end, to reveal His hidden will for this age through His Son. So Christ having prevailed, having conquered and subdued the dominion of the devil in His first advent, He has ascended to the throne so that He might now execute the design of the Father in the purposed conquest of this world and deliverance of His elect in this present age. Seen as the Lion of the tribe of Judah, the offspring of David, we find that Christ is the purposed One to carry out the will of the Father in this age in the advance of the kingdom of heaven to the subduing of the kingdoms on Earth. When John is taken in the spirit to behold what God has planned, little could he know that the Lord had planned to conquer all. It is a cosmic, eternal plan the Lord is conducting, with the designed end of His glory and victory over a fallen and rebellious world.

As the fourth chapter closes, we, like John, have not seen Jesus yet. Where is He? As the fifth chapter opens, the drama is intensified; when shall he appear? And what of the scroll, how shall it be opened? So is prepared that moment of His arising to take and open that which has been sealed. But as he arises, He shall be seen in a way most unexpected. He shall be seen as a Lamb. He shall be a Lamb having seven horns and seven eyes, which are the seven spirits of God. He arises to take the book and open its seals, to complete the eternal design of God. Revelation is not for some future age so that this age might be of no great relevance; rather, this is the age where the risen Lord, the Lamb that is as though slain, having prevailed, loosens the seals of God's foreordained will, which is to conquer and redeem a people to Himself. So advances the narrative. The time has come to begin the next phase of God's design.

Thus, when the Lamb takes the scroll, a new song is sung, the song of conquest and victory, which says, "Thou art worthy to take the book, and to open the seals thereof: for thou wast slain, and hast redeemed us to God by thy blood out of every kindred, and tongue, and people, and nation; And hast made us unto our God kings and priests: and we shall reign on the earth." Because of what He has done in the previous age He now does in this age, which is to conquer and subdue the world before us. For John, who had been exiled and tormented, who was alone in Patmos, what greater hope than to see that the Beast, the False Prophet, and the great Whore had not won, and that the Dragon in all his fury was not to win. What joy must have been his to see that Christ had prevailed, that He ruled, and that He reigns, and we in Him, to the end of the will of God eternal. Chapters 4 and 5 prepare the reader for this hope, knowing that what follows God has willed, God has planned, God has perfectly prepared for us and His Son eternal.

CHAPTER 6

The Lord's Will in This Present Age

The purpose of these next two chapters is to detail how the will of God is designed to be carried out in this present age. It is marvelous to see that nothing has come to pass that the sovereign Lord has not purposed, and that nothing is ever haphazard or capricious, but always for the Lord's glory and our good. Chapter 6 begins with the Lamb opening the first of seven seals. The seals are loosed to reveal the eternal plan of God for this age, which is to conquer this world and redeem His own. Each seal is separate, consecutive, but not chronological, they are inter-laden and comprised of two parts. The first set of seals consist of four seals of similar content, that content containing the Lord's directives to the dictates of divine providence. The ultimate design of each is to cover the Lamb's conquest and advance in this world. Thus, the first of the four seals comprising the first of two sets of seals is of the Lamb conquering this world in this age.

As there are seven seals, it is on account of the age being set in the construct of the likeness of a creation week, a week being not of time, but of design. While the original creation was of seven literal days, this age in prophetic form is likened unto the days of creation, but unlike them as well. For while the first seven days were consecutive and progressive, so the second set are consecutive and progressive, just not in the scope of seven literal days. Some of the events and happenings of the seven seals contained within are continuous and congruous while others are successive, each to its own design. Thus, we must remember that while this age is likened unto a week of creation, it spans the time begun with Christ's departure from earth until His return. Clearly, the Lord chose the motif of creation for two ends; first, to show that the time is short, and second, to show that it is a perfect work of the divine will.

It must not be lost sight of that this is a vision, that this is but that which represents something else. Nothing is as it seems. Horses dispatched from the reading of a king's edict are what is pictured in the first four of seven seals revealed. There are no literal horses or riders. They are not to ride one day upon the earth. But the image is of the will of our eternal God carried out in the dispatches of a Sovereign. He orders and the Lord rides in His glory to accomplish the divine decrees. We must remember that they are also not chronological, as Revelation does not lend itself to a chronological interpretation. The content revealed by the opening of the seals is not consecutive, it is concurrent, and that contained within the scroll is as a whole, containing the will of God sent forth in this age to complete His design. Four riders are seen first upon four horses that ride forth in battle to do what has been ordered. They represent the will of God to be carried out by means of divine providence.

First, one like unto our Lord Himself is seen seated upon a stallion with the dispatch to conquer in His hand. The first seal opens up the content which indicates that this age is an age of conquest. The Lamb sends forth the rider and that rider shall conquer the earth. The same rider is seen again at the end of the prophecy, having completed His labor to conquer conquering. It is our Lord. But since it represents the will of our Lord, it is not literally Him, just He that represents Him. In Revelation 19:11–16, we are given the necessary information to deduce that this first rider is the Lord Himself, as He is the one previously called *faithful and true*, who was described as having eyes as flames of fire, who John will see bearing the name *the Word of God.* He appears in chapter 19 victorious, having His garments stained with the blood of His foes, riding forth to tread the winepress of the wrath of God, as it says,

> And the armies which were in heaven followed him upon white horses, clothed in fine

linen, white and clean. And out of his mouth goeth a sharp sword, that with it he should smite the nations: and he shall rule them with a rod of iron: and he treadeth the winepress of the fierceness and wrath of Almighty God. And he hath on his vesture and on his thigh a name written, KING OF KINGS, AND LORD OF LORDS.

Here, He is seen first as having been given a crown, and riding forth, "conquering, and to conquer." Our Lord, having risen and ascended, having been enthroned on high, as Peter testified at Pentecost,

> This Jesus hath God raised up, whereof we all are witnesses. Therefore being by the right hand of God exalted, and having received of the Father the promise of the Holy Ghost, he hath shed forth this, which ye now see and hear. For David is not ascended into the heavens: but he saith himself, The LORD said unto my Lord, Sit thou on my right hand, Until I make thy foes thy footstool.

Thus, the first seal indicates that this age is the age in which the Father has decreed the conquering and ultimate conquest is of the Son, who starts crowned and enthroned, and ends with many crowns and the name *King of kings and Lord of lords*. So we know, as John and those of his days knew, that what we see around us, what we observe in this world, is the advance of our Lord's kingdom conquering nations by the preached word. This is that foreordained by the eternal council of God.

Furthermore, we see three other aspects of the carrying out of the divine will that bring about that conquest, justice, redemption, and vindication of the Lord's name, and those are in the subsequent horses. The first is the second seal, which indicates war, war ordained of the Lord, whereby men in their own vile lusts and passions make war, all within the scheme and design of God. The Lord has decreed that there should be the directives of divine providence superintending the unrest on earth. As it says, to this rider is granted the means "to take peace from the earth, and that they should kill one another: and there was given unto him a great sword." Wherever we see warfare on earth, wherever there is violence and death, we know that it is of the Lord, to the end of His glory, our deliverance, and the execution of His wrath. This age is an age of war; men wage war of their own volition, but that volition is governed and directed by the sovereign hand of God. Thus, we can know that wars, while vile and repulsive, are under the oversight and direction of God. The third horseman directs famine, the fourth death. Altogether, we see that all that occurs below, though brought about by the passions of men, are under the design and directive of the God of heaven and earth, unto the end of the completed conquest and victory of our Lord.

Where there are wars, where there is striving, where there is death, we know that it is as God has decreed. This world is in rebellion against our God. He has decreed its punishment, He has ordered a blessed redemption, He is executing the fierceness of His wrath, and everything that transpires is purposed of God, directed of God, and designed to the end of His foreordained purpose, that He might redeem a people to Himself so that He might judge the world in righteousness, and in the end, restore that which was lost unto His ultimate glory. All that men endure, famine, dearth, death, and war, all are in this age designed of God to His ends. This is what the Lord willed long ago, that those living in this world, chosen of God, elect of the Father, given to the Son, who have endured such hardships, shall be preserved through great tribulations in this age, all as the Lord has willed, to the end that He shall subdue the earth and conquer this world. As a Sovereign, He has decreed that His will shall send forth at once justice and mercy, amidst the chaos of this world, to the end He has purposed. There are days when wars rage, others where famines strike, times when plagues and death abound, at times more than others, at other times not at all, but throughout this age the Lord has willed that they shall come.

Yet this is not all, despite the full scope of the will of God and the execution of His purpose seen in the first four riders, we find that the seals of the decrees of the Lord contain more detail. Each of the successive revelations in this book will follow this same pattern of three separate parts, in order to unveil each manifested revelation. First, there will be a general view of the Lord's work in this age upon the earth, where the Lord's conquest is detailed amidst the constructs of this world. Then will follow a specific portion where the reader's attention is drawn to either the visible church and/or the true church. Finally, the end and its drawing near will be shown; then the end comes. Here then, after the first four seals, three remain; the first four seals overview the Lord's conquest in this age by means of the various afflictions of providence, and the final three seals revealing that which finalizes the design of God. After the first set of seals are opened, the second set of seals are opened to reveal the ultimate end of the Lord for this age. It is His design to deliver His people and to judge the earth.

Thus, the fifth seal shows the plight of the people of the Lord in persecution, the sixth seal details the drawing near of the day of the Lord, and the last seal unveils the end of it all. This pattern repeats itself in the three revelations of the things of this age. Therefore, we see in the fifth seal that a special category always exists in this age for those persecuted for the Word of God. Persecution is that which the Lord has ordained for His elect in this present age; ours is a cross before us. The reason is that the Lord and the world's ruler are at war. Two kingdoms are in conflict. The world and its allies are enraged and united against our Lord and His elect. In this age the Lord has ordained that those that suffer shall be comforted. Though they perish, they reign, as was promised, He "hath made us kings and priests unto God and his Father." As this book is for the chief end of the comfort of the saints, for our use in this age of persecution and furious warfare, we find that those that are put to the sword have not been forgotten. It is the will of God that they have died, but it is also the will of God that they are near to Him, to be dressed in white, and promised that their plight is only for a short time. What those in John's day were suffering was not then without hope; instead, they could trust that it was of the will of God that through their death they should reign, like Christ before them. He shall keep them close. He shall comfort them and cloth them. He shall say to them, "Rest yet for a little season."

As then, the first four seals had no chronological organization, neither do the final three. Each one is categorical. Each subsequently detailing God's ordained design of this age. The first four spoke to the employment of general providence in the coming conquest of His kingdom. The fifth demonstrating His especial care for His elect that perish. The sixth the coming end of the age. And the seventh seal unveiling the end itself. Altogether, all seven summarize the work of God in this age amidst the directives of divine providence and our Lord's governance of this world. He brings all things to pass.

The sixth seal addresses the end of the age, just as each subsequent revelation makes this distinction as well. The sixth trumpet heralds the coming of the end. And the angel flying through heaven announces the end. In all three views of the design of this age, each ends with the drawing near of the end. The coming of the Lord is detailed and then the consequence of that coming is delineated. Each time it is sudden, not drawn out, and the end is swift and final. Each time a distinction is made between those of the world and those chosen of the Lord. The sixth seal employs prophetic language indicative of the day of the Lord. As in past prophecies, the day of the Lord is cataclysmic. It is universal in scope. It comes without warning. It is calamitous. All that the Lord has created is shaken, the heavens and earth upheave, and the Lord appears. The world is terrorized at His appearing. The whole earth and its inhabitants that remain are called to account. In this case, the sixth seal reveals that those of the world seek to escape His appearing with no success. Every hiding place is removed. Every man is called to account. Notice that there are no signs of the end given or spoken of in this revelation. Notice that when the day appears it is sudden, the Lord's own are removed, and those remaining are brought to account. No man escapes, whether king or beggar, religious or irreligious, rich or poor, none can escape His wrath, as we hear, "For the great day of his wrath is come; and who shall be able to stand?" All that remain that are not the Lord's shall in that day be judged.

Therefore, see what the sixth seal teaches us. There are no events that precede the coming of the Lord. The will of God from eternity is that in this age there will be various manifestations of wars, famines, dearth, and death, as the world persecutes those chosen of the Lord. All the while He is plundering the nations, conquering kingdoms, and advancing His glory and will. But when the day comes, it comes with suddenness and finality, and those on the earth will be stricken with fear, for their end has come. But there will be no drawn-out battles and engagements; instead, when the Lamb of God appears, it shall be done. This pattern of suddenness is proven over and again through this book. There is but one return of Christ and it comes without warning. There is but one day of the Lord remaining. It is ordained of God. No signs proceed it. There will be no great manifestation of trouble before His return nor elongated periods of peace proceeding that day, but when it comes, it comes.

The seventh seal of Revelation is brief. The loosening of the first seal revealed the crowned and mounted Lord riding forth in battle. The subsequent three seals revealed the Lord's orchestration of providence in this present age. The fifth seal reassured us of our salvation in Him. The sixth prepared the world for His sudden and unexpected coming. This is the age of conquest. During this conquest there will be wars, famines, dearth, and death, coming in various stages and manifestations. Saints will perish but they will reign. Yes, the time is short, as the Lord tells those slain for His word, "Rest yet for a little season." So they are called to wait, to wait for those yet to join them as it is ordained. And when the end comes, it comes, and all things shall be complete. As the seventh seal is loosened, it is loosened to show that in the end it shall be finished; the Lord's eternal work, which like the first work of creation, shall end when He is done. As we read, God has willed a final day for rest and reflection upon the Lord's glorious work, just as He did in the beginning. Here we find a final sabbath is decreed for the end of this age. The world will be upheaved, men will be called to account, and all that made war with Him and His elect shall not escape. Unlike the first sabbath day, this is merely spoken of as a type. As that first sabbath brought an end and glorious reflection upon the Lord's work, so shall the end of this age come with finality. All the Lord has willed shall be done, and being done, it will be glorious and perfect, more so than the first of sabbaths. For the world, their end will come, and as their end comes in sorrow, the elect of the Lord, the bride of Christ, His Israel, she shall be saved. They shall all accounted be accounted for and delivered. Then, all shall reflect upon His glory and perfect work.

All in all, the seven seals show us that this age, the second age, is foreordained of the Lord, and all that comes to pass is of His design. It is perfect, glorious, salvific, and just, and when it is said and done, none shall doubt His righteousness and glory. For the saints of John's day, what a glorious picture to behold. This portion of Revelation is as its own Genesis. It details the Lord's sovereign will in the created order, His covenantal grace and purposed redemption for His elect, the certain justice due to all those fallen in Adam, and an end certain to display His incomparable and impeccable glory. John was blessed to observe what God had written. He was blessed to take it from the sovereign hand of the Savior and convey its contents to the church. All so we might rest in Him and trust that nothing is outside His will, that all is of His hand, and as such, it shall be perfect in the end, leading us to rest forever in Him. As the final seal is loosed, that place that has never been silenced is silenced. Heaven, which forever is heard filled with the sovereign Lord's praise, can but stop, wonder, and behold the full and complete glory of the godhead in this age and the past, unto a perfect end. How best to end it all with heaven silenced for but half an hour. The time tells us that it is certain, but yet incomplete; for the book of Revelation is not complete.

CHAPTER 7

SEALING THE LORD'S ELECT

Before the final seal is opened, the seventh chapter is introduced as an interlude between the sixth and seventh seals. It continues the revelation of the Lord's eternal will at the completion of this age. It is in this chapter that the apostle's attention is drawn to the sanctifying of the Lord's elect. While the world flees the coming of the Lord time is stopped in order to protect the Lord's people from the catastrophe to come. Four angels are seen staying the winds of the earth, as though time were to stand still so that another angel could announce the sealing of the Lord's elect with His mark. This sixth seal is opened to reveal that which is set in stark contrast to that revealed by the fifth seal. While the inhabitants of the world are seen scurrying and fleeing the approach of the day of the Lord, the angels are dispatched to seal and mark those to be set apart unto the Lord. Time is not relevant to this vision, as again this is not chronological, but thematic, as those of the earth flee the Lord's approaching day, the Lord's chosen are marked, sealed, and set apart to be counted on that special day. It is on that day that the full account of God's will is to be manifest in the judgment of the world and the ingathering of His full church. Again, this is symbolic, representing the will of the Lord to judge the earth and save His own, and it merely is detailed to show the Lord's especial care for His people.

The winds appear to represent the totality of movement and action on the earth; as the winds are stayed, it is as if time stands still, it is as if the wrath of God pauses while those of the earth flee, all so that the gathering of all God's chosen can be assured. Remember, these are not consecutive events, but concurrent, in that while the Lord has decreed through this age famine, war, dearth and death, and the deliverance and kept guard of those slain for His word, He also has been sure to hold back His fury until the time that a full census and accounting of Israel has occurred, until the bride is readied, until the woman of His choice is prepared, then shall time be fully reckoned. Here, then, is but a theatrical chapter that portrays the numbering of the Lord's elect, from start to finish, from the first to the last, accounting for all those of the past age and those of this age, assuring that all of those sealed and marked as the chosen of the Lord are safe.

The angel's declaration, "Hurt not the earth, neither the sea, nor the trees, till we have sealed the servants of our God in their foreheads," is a recitation of the covenant promise of God, likened unto that in Noah's day, seen in the rainbow above the throne, by which the hand of justice is stayed until the ingathering of all the elect. These things of the *earth* are more than just the dressings of creation; they are the social and governmental strictures of this world, the kingdoms of this world and all its machinations, which are not destroyed and done asunder, until the Lord's own are accounted for one and all. So if John was to ask along with the martyrs before God's throne, "How long O Lord?" The answer is here, until all His own are sealed. If we were to ask, why is the Lord stayed yet in heaven? Why has He not judged the ungodly? The answer is simple; it is His purpose to seal, to mark, and account for the deliverance of all His chosen.

So once more, for clarity, this seventh chapter shows us that the image John sees of the angels holding back the winds is but illustrative; it is to show him how the Lord's judicious will is being restrained until the full numbering of Israel is complete. It happens during this age, and throughout this age, the Lord is gathering His saints. Those sealed include those of the past age, along with those of the present age, and it shall include all those throughout this advancing age, until the end, when the day of the Lord shall come, and all the elect of God shall be found safe. Thus, the seventh chapter serves as an interlude to highlight the Lord's especial care for His own. It illustrates that the approaching day of the Lord is paused until all are accounted for. And while the inhabitants of the Earth throughout this age seek to avoid that day, kings, wealthy men, and mighty men, and all those not sealed unto the Lord, are as men fleeing into the rocks dens and mountains to escape that day, yet without success. For when the final census is complete, their end shall come.

Chapter 7 is given to show us the especial care and attention the Lord has placed upon His own. He stays the destructive winds of justice until we are safe, as Ramsey says, "Winds here (ἄνεμος) mean not the gentle and refreshing breezes, but the hurricanes that sweep all before them with ruin, and spread complete desolation in their path. They thus represent all the violent and resistless powers and influences which, when let loose, are to sweep over the earth, and involve it in the ruin just depicted in the previous scene" (325), God tarries for the purpose of gathering His beloved. It is when the number is complete that this shall end. John hears the calling out of the census of God's elect, much like Moses heard so long ago, when the Lord said, "Take ye the sum of all the congregation of the children of Israel" (Num. 1:2). Here though it is a full census of all those sealed, each and every one taken from the earth, summed up as *one hundred and forty-four thousand of all the tribes of the children of Israel.* The will of God summed up in this chapter is to stay the winds of destruction while the Lord intends to mark, gather, and account for all the children of Israel, from first to last so that all Israel shall be saved, the true Israel of God.

Who is Israel? It is not Israel of the flesh, though those that are Israelites of the flesh are included in that number. Instead, it is the Israel of the Spirit, not the circumcised in the flesh, but the circumcised of the heart, as Paul says in Romans 9, "For they are not all Israel, which are of Israel," and it is stated here in the seventh chapter, "A great multitude, which no man could number, of all nations, and kindreds, and people, and tongues," these are Jews and Gentiles, all alike, making up a whole people, agreeing with the consensus here that a full accounting of the Israel of God shall be complete, as Paul says, "All Israel shall be saved." A perfect number, a complete census is taken, much as it was in Moses' day, where then they numbered by the thousands, as it says in Numbers 1:16, "Heads of thousands in Israel." Then, Israel was counted by a representative thousand, which here, including the representative numbers of the twelve patriarchs and twelve apostles, accumulates to one hundred and forty-four thousand. In all, this number, like all numbers in Revelation is symbolic, meant to represent a truth, which here is the full church, all Israel, the woman with all her children, from first to last all God's elect.

Further proof is found in the delineation of the representative tribes of Israel. Those listed here in Revelation 7 are not the original sons of Jacob, nor are they a later synopsis of the tribes, but they are a group chosen to make a point; the point is that the apostate, rebellious, and idolatrous are left out. Judah is first, as should be, as he represents that special elect son from which the line descended. Oddly, Joseph and one of his sons are listed, but the abominable one Ephraim is omitted. Also left out is apostate Dan, who along with Ephraim are representative of the apostate tribes of Israel. So in the end, an odd ordering is not so odd, and a peculiar naming is not so peculiar, as that census including some not originally of the whole, is given to make up a consensus of final Israel. True Israel includes peoples from every nation, kindred, and tongue, as prophesied in Isaiah, "Enlarge the place of thy tent, and let them stretch forth the curtains of thine habitations: spare not, lengthen thy cords, and strengthen thy stakes; For thou shalt break forth on the right hand and on the left; and thy seed shall inherit the Gentiles, and make the desolate cities to be inhabited" (Isa. 54:2–3), but excluded are the idolatrous and apostates. What we have in Revelation 7 is a *representative* census of the elect of God, designated as Israel, reordered and absent the apostate, filled with peoples of the Gentiles, comprising all the elect, sealed of God, from first to last, she is Israel, so that it is as Paul says, "All Israel shall be saved," a great multitude, which no man could number, of all nations, and kindreds, and people, and tongues, who are heard proclaiming, "Salvation to our God which sitteth upon the throne, and unto the Lamb." Here is Israel, God's elect, from first to last, shown sealed and delivered, in contrast to those of the earth who flee, seeking to escape the judgment to come. God's will has always been for the salvation and deliverance of His covenant people. They are Abraham's children. They are Israel. They include those Gentiles that are grafted into the stock of Jacob. So that in the end, all Israel shall be saved.

What a glorious sight for John to see that day. For while he was exiled, while he was perplexed, living during a day of great tribulation and persecution, during which he of all the apostles stood alone, he was afforded great confidence and joy by beholding this vision, knowing that none are to be lost, that all are to be saved, and that in the end they shall all stand and shout to the Lord, "Hosannah, save now O Lord!" John gets to see that which represents the full eternal will of God in redeeming a people to Himself. He gets to see the bride of the Lamb fully arrayed in the Lord's righteousness and splendor. He gets to see her standing purified in Him, clothed in white, saying, "Amen: Blessing, and glory, and wisdom, and thanksgiving, and honour, and power, and might, be unto our God for ever and ever. Amen." Despite all John has seen below, above he now sees that the Lord has willed otherwise. None are lost, hope is not given way to dismay, but the Lord has decreed the salvation of His elect, their full and final deliverance, and in the end, the Lord shall be shown faithful.

At the end of this census comes a final aside, while John is beholding the true decretive will of redemption for Israel his attention is drawn away, as he is asked by an elder, "What are these which are arrayed in white robes? and whence came they?" Designed to have John declare, "Sir, thou knowest," it is the Lord's intent to provide this further insight into that stated in chapter 1, "He hath made us kings and priests unto God and his Father." John, coming from thirty years of great tribulation and suffering, where he has been exiled and tortured, during which he has seen his fellow apostles and brethren slain by the Beast, he is here afforded this comfort in knowing that those slain are presently reigning in heaven above, as the elder says,

> These are they which came out of great trib-
> ulation, and have washed their robes, and made

them white in the blood of the Lamb. Therefore are they before the throne of God, and serve him day and night in his temple: and he that sitteth on the throne shall dwell among them. They shall hunger no more, neither thirst any more; neither shall the sun light on them, nor any heat. For the Lamb which is in the midst of the throne shall feed them, and shall lead them unto living fountains of waters: and God shall wipe away all tears from their eyes.

What a glorious end to it all, for John to see that those he knew and those yet to come, who shall be slain by the Beast and False Prophet, who shall be abused by the Whore and the Dragon, are yet reigning with the Lamb above. Revelation is after all a glorious picture of the felicity and peace of heaven above granted those of the Lamb that reign in and with Him there, in contradistinction to the turmoil, suffering, and plight on the earth, for those driven by the Dragon to blasphemy and ruin. This the Lord has decreed. By way of the opening of the seals, this is now known and unsealed, though not yet complete. From the first to the sixth seal, we find that all that is, it comes from the design and will of God. It is He who brings all things to pass, it is He that intends to judge the earth and its habitants, who intends to save and deliver His own, so that they might reign with Him forever. It is He who throughout this age is directing all things to this final end, which as it approaches echoes doom to the world, but joy to those to reign with Him above, it is as Ramsey says, "Jesus Christ reigns, is the grand lesson of the seven-sealed book; reigns in all gospel agencies; in war, in want, in death, and in the sufferings of the martyrs; and is in all these only overturning the world, sealing His chosen, and so gathering His redeemed around His throne" (353). What follows all this? Silence.

Chapter 8 begins with the end of this first vision. It is the seventh seal that opens to reveal that it all ends in silence. Like God in six days created heaven and earth; he shaped and filled it and called it *very good,* so shall the end of this age come with equal pause and glory. Our Lord shall in that day usher in a new, final sabbath rest, and when all shall be done, it shall be declared good. Verse 1 of chapter 8 belongs with chapter 7. It is brief and final. It shows that when a full census of all Israel is taken, when all the elect are accounted for, then shall the day of the Lord come. Then shall come the end, and when it comes, all the turmoil before it, all the suffering of those having endured it, shall be finished, and all those waiting shall find that God's work shall be finished.

Like the first sabbath so the last day is likened as a day of silence. Both in heaven and on earth, when all is said and done, it shall be known that the Lord's will shall be complete; there will be no more to be completed. All is to be said and done. It is here likened unto a sabbath in heaven. Here the end is represented by a half hour silence in heaven. As all pause to behold what the Lord has done, to consider what He has finished, to marvel over His completed work, then shall everyone know and affirm that He is just, merciful, and glorious. They shall know He is the Lord God Almighty. They shall know Him as faithful and true. With the final seal opened, there is nothing more to reveal. His sealed will is revealed to be complete. What He purposed shall be done. Remember, Revelation is symbolic, and here is represented that final sabbath, which is long in heaven, but short in duration.

One might ask, when has heaven ever been silent? Never. But now, now that all is known, now that we see like John all that God has decreed, now that we behold the wonders of His glory, what else could we do but pause in silence? Silence, as the earth and all its fury and turmoil are silenced. Silence as in heaven all stand to behold the wonders of God's eternal will. As the first of three visions of the *things yet to come* closes, we find that this first vision informs us that all things are done in accordance with the divine council of God. He has written the days, foreordained the age, and designed the course of history. He has bookended the two ages with Christ's two advents. Christ is decreed to advance His glory, honor, and kingdom, redeeming His own, and judging the world in righteousness.

The reader of John's day, as the apostle himself, could take great comfort in knowing that all things are according to the design and purpose of the Almighty. The chaos and terror they knew was not haphazard nor capricious; they were not at the whims of their foes. God the Father, through His Son our Lord, has been orchestrating a plan so merciful and glorious, that no man could have imagined it. We now know that throughout this age there shall be famines, wars, we shall want, and death shall come, but all that is sent, all that is dispatched, is of heaven, to the purpose of advancing His kingdom and delivering His own safe to the uttermost while riding forth conquering to conquer. Christ reigns to plunder the earth! Christ the Lamb of God rides forth amidst the harrowing plights of this life to redeem His own and deliver this world to judgment. He truly is the Alpha and Omega. As the age begins with Him installed as King, it ends with His return. It is an age likened unto a week, whereby God has predestined all things to the end of His glory and our salvation, which, in the end, shall prove far more glorious than that of the first creative week. As silence figuratively ends the first vision of the *things which shall be*, it ends our doubts. As heaven pauses for the one and only moment in all time, we find that heaven and earth paused merely to behold the true glory and sovereign design of the Almighty. As the first vision closes, you can almost hear the words of Moses in Genesis 1:31 echoed, "And God saw everything that he had made, and, behold, it was very good."

CHAPTERS 8–11

AN OVERVIEW OF HEAVEN'S KINGDOM'S ADVANCE AND THE WORLD'S CONQUEST

Here begins the second division of that Christ identified as that *which is to come*. The focus of this section is conquest. Thus, trumpets are sounded to send forth the messengers, to enlist the warriors, and prepare the events that are to transpire throughout this age, until the final conquest is complete. There is an undeniable similarity between what is found in the opening of the seals and the pouring out of the bowls of the Lord's wrath. These patterns are similar, and while similar, the content is not. Where the seals focus upon the eternal design and sovereign will of God, and later, the bowls will look to the wrath and judgment of the Lord, the trumpets of this second division look to the advance of the kingdom of heaven and the subsequent conquest of the kingdoms of this world. Here, the focus is upon victory.

This is the age of conquest. In the past age, a heritage was made, made to prepare the day for the coming of the Son of God, who would come forth to conquer the world. The previous age was the age of promise. In Abraham, we were promised a seed. In Abraham, we were promised a heritage. In Abraham, we were promised a land eternal. In Abraham, we were promised that God would be our God. But in Abraham, we were shown to be pilgrims and strangers on the earth. Ours was a covenant of promise, ours a covenant of grace. As a type, the promises of old prefigured our day, the day in which Christ our redeemer would complete all that was foreshadowed in promises.

That which was in type is now to be realized in Christ our Lord. This is the age of fulfilment. That which was in type is now to be realized in Christ our Lord. This is the age of fulfilment.

Similarly, the kingdom of Israel prefigured the conquest Christ the Lord would bring; He would be our Joshua, indicative of the meaning of the names Joshua and Jesus, "the Lord saves," this was the name which our Lord was given from heaven. He would save His people from their sins. He would rule His people. He would bring us peace. He would drive forth the nations before us. He would set up His authority in heaven and on earth. In Moses, He would lead us from bondage to our evil taskmaster. He would lead us from our sins. In David, we see our Lord as our deliverer, who would subdue our enemies and deliver us from bondage to our foes. In Solomon, He would be our beloved, He would embody the wisdom of God, and He would bring lasting peace.

Christ has ascended on high. He has led captivity captive. He has given gifts to men. In this next section that spans to the end of the eleventh chapter, we will find that the Lord's attention is upon conquest. He has conquered our sin, now He endeavors to subdue all our foes. Already He has wounded our chief enemy. Already He has stricken our foe. Already He has bound the devil. Already He has curtailed his reach. This is the age of advance. This is the age of plunder. Christ is advancing His kingdom. He is plundering the nations of this world. All by the power of His word. What was begun at Pentecost with the pouring out of the Spirit and the adding of three thousand to heaven's roles, Christ is continuing to the ends of the earth.

In the next section, John shall be shown the manner in which Christ makes war, how He subdues the nations, and how He shall in this age overcome our foes. Again, set within the construct of 7, this time employing the image of trumpets rather than seals, the focus will be upon warfare and success. Like it was with the seals, the seven trumpets are divided into two parts; the first part consists of four trumpets, all of which allude to the engagements our Lord faces against the forces of this world. The final three trumpets will follow the same pattern as the seals, focusing upon the coming day of the

Lord and the resilience of His forces here below. Altogether, this section is best summed up with this that is prophesied in the end, "The kingdoms of this world are become the kingdoms of our Lord, and of his Christ; and he shall reign for ever and ever." If one were to ask, "What is the point of this portion of Revelation?" The answer would be this verse, as this is the goal of this vision.

Chapter 8: Heavenly Warfare and Conquest

Beginning with verse 2, chapter 8 introduces us to the next categorical explanation of this age. This next view of this present age is from the perspective of warfare, and it encompasses the eighth through eleventh chapters. Trumpet blasts proceed the advance of the kingdom of heaven. Hendriksen calls them "trumpets of judgment." I deem these blasts of the host of heaven upon the horn as the means by which the Lord sends forth His forces to upset and overcome the world. Much like the trumpets of Israel that would sound in battle, so these trumpets sound. Remember how the trumpets sounded at Jericho when the walls fell. Remember how the trumpets of Gideon sounded the Midianites' defeat. These trumpets in Revelation are like those, heralds of the advance of the Lord's reign and the fall of the walls of Satan's kingdom.

Knowing, therefore, that this age is designed by the eternal council of God to be an age of certain conquest, we now add to that knowledge both understanding and confidence that our Lord shall prevail. This age is the age wherein the Lamb of God rides forth to conquer. He is to be seen in this vision conquering worldly societies, governments, and economic powers, and He is seen overcoming such forces without and within the visible church, until the final trumpet affirms these words, "The kingdoms of this world are become the kingdoms of our Lord, and of his Christ; and he shall reign for ever and ever." This declaration is heralded at the start of the age, and it is affirmed at its end. As Jesus said to His disciples in the Upper Room, "I have overcome the world," so now He rides forth to conquer by His blood.

Embedded within this book is the notion that what is has already been and is coming to pass, the already but not yet tension of Revelation, whereby the certainty of the end is affirmed, but the finality of it is quickly approaching. Thus, like Israel was given Canaan by the Lord before they ever owned it, so Christ is said to have conquered the world, even before that conquest is finally complete. Even though the Lord had promised Israel the land of Canaan, they still had to advance and conquer it. So Christ has overcome the world, but as scripture testifies, the Father has said to His Son, "Sit on my right hand, until I make thine enemies thy footstool" (Heb. 1:13). What is declared in heaven is as if it has already been done. What is started in God's promises on earth are equally sure. When God makes a promise, the outcome of that promise is certain. It can be stated as though it has already come to pass. Thus, much of what John hears and sees contains this tension; it is declared as though it is done while yet it is not complete. This tension pervades the whole of Revelation.

As we pass the momentary half-hour of silence in heaven, it is interrupted by the next vision given the apostle. As each successive vision in Revelation proceeds from the throne of God, so does this second of three. Keeping in mind that seven is the construct of the visions of the *things to come* in Revelation, we see "next seven angels which stood before God; and to them were given seven trumpets." What John is to see is not like that seen before; remember, Revelation is not chronological, but thematic, as Hendriksen says, "The trumpets are synchronous with the seals" (116). So we are not to observe in the trumpets what follows the opening of the seals. Instead, what will be declared by the trumpets is like that which was made known by the seals, only the *perspective* has changed. Consider it like the four Gospels; they all tell of the same information, but from a different vantage point. So it is with these three visions of that which is to come, we are observing with John different aspects of the things that come to pass in this age.

As before, John observed that the Lord was the sovereign designer of this age of conquest, now John will see that the Lord is He that goes forth to subdue the world. He will not be thwarted;

His will shall be done. None stand in His way. What is sounded and dispatched in heaven is brought to pass. If it is heard in heaven, it is certain to come to pass on Earth. The Lord reigns in righteousness and glory, as from the throne of heaven He rules, so that the "kingdom of the world shall become the kingdoms of our Lord, and of His Christ, and He shall reign for ever and ever." So it is from heaven that all things proceed and advance to this end. What God decreed is now brought to pass, by His sovereign providence He sounds the advance of His glory and reign, dispatching angels, messengers of heaven, to make known what the Lord shall bring to pass.

Yet before the first trumpet sounds, another angel comes forth to tend to the altar. It is the altar of incense. This may be an angel dispatched from our Lord, who like our High Priest, sends forth an angel to intercede and ready our prayers. It is best to not try to identify every angel, but rather to consider what that angel represents. John sees an angel; his task is to tend to the altar. So with a golden censer he draws from the altar incense and fire and casts it to the earth, demonstrating the usefulness of the prayers of the saints in this present age. This action symbolizes the pleasure and use of our prayers to the design of God's glory.

What a glorious blessing for John to behold. Remember what the purpose of this book is, it is for us to be blessed, they "that readeth, and they that hear the words of this prophecy, and keep those things which are written therein." And what better for that blessedness to be had by them who behold the use of their prayers in heaven to shake the earth below. Recall that everything in this book is symbolic. The altar represents a repository of the prayers of the saints kept near the throne of God. The action represents how our prayers are employed by the Lord for His purpose. Together, these actions and this image emboldens the hearts of the downtrodden and persecuted, to know that our pleas are not in vain. The fact that these prayers and coals are cast to the earth demonstrates that they are used of the Lord to shake the earth, as they produce "voices, and thunderings, and lightnings, and an earthquake." What a glorious image for us who are said to *reign with Christ*, that know that our troubles and pleas are not in vain but are used of the Lord to advance His glory on earth. With this emboldening image John is poised to now watch as the trumpets sound to advance the warfare of the Lamb from heaven to the earth. From the throne to the angels, from the angels to the altar, from the altar to the angels again, they are seen preparing themselves to sound. They, having paused for the intercession of the angel, who is given to ready our prayers, they now step forth to carry out their mission.

The first angel sounds his trumpet, and like the seals, we find there is great congruity between what was shown with the first four seals and what is shown with the first four trumpets. In fact, there is great similarity between the seven occurrences of the seals, trumpets, and bowls, all of which provide separate perspectives of the happenings of God's sovereign providence in this age. So keeping this in mind, the first four angels sound their trumpets in succession, not in time, but merely in sequence. Each sound produces a separate event. Together, they bring about a singular purpose. They announce the woes of conquest and judgment to the earth below, which is to be conducted throughout this age. The woes are to come upon the world and its kings and kingdoms. By the trumpet blasts, the Lord brings proportionate calamities upon this world. Societies are upset, commerce in this world is plagued, and the collusion of nations occurs, all the while kingdoms are undone. These events are repetitious and congruous throughout this age. Like the first four seals demonstrated that the Lord has ordained judgment to this age for the earth in the form of death, warfare, violence, and dearth, so here we find that He advances His sovereign providence to upset the world and its order.

The first trumpet is said to scorch a third of the earth itself. Recalling that everything in Revelation is symbolic, we remember that trees and seas represent more than mere trees and oceans. Simply, if one-third of the earth itself was subsequently scorched and devoured by these judgments, nothing would be left to destroy by the time Revelation ends. All things are figurative. Numbers are symbolic, items are symbolic, everything is representative of that which it represents. Therefore, when we read, "Hail and fire mingled with blood, and they were cast upon the earth: and the third part of trees was burnt up, and all green grass was burnt up," we are not to conclude that one day the Lord will send actual fire and hail to burn up a third of the earth's vegetation, instead we are to look for the meaning behind this symbol. Ramsey likens this to, "The productions of the earth; and hence can represent only the benefits growing out of such a state of consolidated social order, as the regular administration of laws by civil rulers; and the security, wealth, and thousand enjoyments of social life and civilization" (371). What we find then is that through this age the Lord shall by His sovereign providence upset, unrest, upheave, and destroy all that kings and kingdoms here below seek to establish in the order of society. Like Babel in Genesis 11, the Lord shall send a blast of His nostrils to scatter men, disturb their comforts, and unsettle their accomplishments, He works against them, as it is the Lord that has ordained their end. This first of trumpets shows us that the Lord from heaven upsets the combined efforts of men here below, in their societies, governments, and commerce. And his judgments are proportionate, as but a third are harmed, with the purpose of distressing and unsettling them, until the day of their final demise comes to be.

The second trumpet looks to another part of the world's order, kingdoms which fall, where are "as it were a great mountain burning with fire was cast into the sea: and the third part of the sea became blood," and as they fall the Lord's kingdom is established. Here we find mountains represent kingdoms. This was so in Old Testament prophesies, where mountains were likened unto kingdoms. Isaiah prophesied of this truth, saying, "And it shall come to pass in the last days, that the mountain of the LORD'S house shall be established in the top of the mountains, and shall be exalted above the hills; and all nations shall flow unto it" (Isa. 2:2). So here we see how the kingdoms of this world that rise up are likened unto mountains, which are torn down from the Lord on high, in order to advance His kingdom. The sea, representing the mass of humanity, consumes that which was a kingdom, and the blood of that kingdom is mingled with the sea. This shows us that kingdoms in this age rise and fall, all to the end the Lord has determined, which in the end is His conquest of all nations. Again, the fall of nations is proportionate, as they will not be finally subdued until the end; thus, the measurement of a third.

With the third trumpet "there fell a great star from heaven, burning as it were a lamp, and it fell upon the third part of the rivers, and upon the fountains of waters; And the name of the star is called Wormwood." Here is pictured the commerce and trade of the nations, which suffer from the blast of the trumpet of God's wrath, again, each being proportionately stricken, demonstrating that throughout this age the earth's security, trade, commerce, wealth, and kingdoms, are stricken and laid low by the divine providence of God as He works His will. How often the imperceptible providence of God makes life bitter for this hostile world.

Last, from the fourth trumpet, the "sun was smitten, and the third part of the moon, and the third part of the stars; so as the third part of them was darkened, and the day shone not for a third part of it, and the night likewise," showing that the truth of heaven, knowledge, and wisdom, is equally through this age proportionately to be veiled. The truth of the Lord, His influence on earth, is that which benefits the nations. As His truth is veiled, as His name is stricken from the minds of men, as His law and order are taken from their consciences, they suffer. Through this age, the Lord's truth is often constrained to leave the world dark. Altogether, parallel in form and type to the first four seals, these trumpets address the social, worldly order of kingdom's, nations, trade, and commerce, and all that is reaped from this earth, which will be stricken and smitten by the blast of the Sovereign's trumpet, only proportionate, but immense, as the Lord withholds the true and lasting recompense of His wrath until the end.

As the eighth chapter closes, a remarkable sight appears, knowing the horror of that which has already seen pales in comparison from that what is to come, an angel appears to startle those in heaven, saying, "With a loud voice, Woe, woe, woe, to the inhabiters of the earth by reason of the other voices of the trumpet of the three angels, which are yet to sound!" The Lord's sovereign, proportionate expunging of His wrath through this age is sufficient to marvel heaven and earth, but more is yet to come, and it will incrementally increase the wonder of all that behold it. The wrath and thunderous conquest of the King of kings and Lord of lords is incomprehensible.

Three woes are yet to come, as if what were yet was not enough, yet what is to come will far eclipse the wonder of that which was before. John is to stand and watch the wonder of the Lord's divine order, which proceeds from heaven to earth, to judge and upset the earth, while displaying His glory and justice, mingled with mercy, and this is marvelous. Notice that it is the *inhabitants of the earth* that the woes are sounded unto, for they are yet to suffer more. All that John has seen is of the Lord. Its design is His glory, deliverance, and justice, which is wondrous to behold.

Chapter 9: The Coming Day of the Lord's Conquest

As the angel proclaimed, the last three trumpets are woes of judgment, and while the first four trumpets were blasts of the Lord's conquering might and vengeance, still, these last three will make the former blasts pale in comparison to these latter proclamations. Much like that evidenced by the final three seals, these three woes follow the similar pattern; they show the coming day of the Lord in judgment, the Lord ushering His own into life eternal, and the world being brought to judgment. The context continues to address the world's structures, orders, governments, and commerce, all as the Lord advances to lay low His adversaries. It is important to realize that another type is here being employed by the Lord to show forth His bringing of pestilence to the earth. The ten plagues of Egypt are the shadows employed to illustrate the Lord's plagues of judgment upon this world. This said, these last three trumpets complete the revelation of the Lord's call to upset the earth and advance His kingdom to victory.

The fifth trumpet's blast brings John's attention to a falling star from heaven. It is not a literal star, but an allusion to an event that will be shown thrice over in the latter part of Revelation; it is the symbolic fall of Satan from heaven to earth. This is not that fall of Satan at the beginning, which many have errantly taught and believed since the Middle Ages, which in and of itself is not biblically supported. Scripture does not teach that Satan fell from heaven prior to the coming of Christ in His first advent. Calvin affirms this repeatedly, as is seen in his comments on Isaiah 14. There it is said that Lucifer fell, of which Calvin says, "Yet it was an instance of very gross ignorance, to imagine that Lucifer was the king of devils, and that the Prophet gave him this name. But as these inventions have no probability whatever, let us pass by them as useless fables" (Commentaries: Isa. 14:12). Old fables are often hard to dispel. What we are seeing now in the fifth trumpet is the event that ushered in this age, the judgment of Satan. What John hears is that which Jesus spoke of when He said, "I beheld Satan as lightning fall from heaven" (Luke 10:18). In Luke, Christ was speaking of the sending out of His disciples and the effect it had upon the prince of this world; as the kingdom of our Lord advances, he that is our accuser and enemy is judged. Here, we are observing the similar construct; as the kingdom of heaven advances, Satan is judged.

Therefore, this star falling from heaven that accompanies the fifth trumpet is indicative of Satan's judgment at the cross, coming with the rising of our Lord and his ascension to the throne, whereby Satan was judged and cast from heaven. It is imperative to remain objective here. Satan is no more a star than the angels or ministers called *stars* by our Lord in chapter 1 were stars. Similarly, to say that Satan was cast from heaven is in itself too simplistic. As Satan is not corporeal, how then can he be restricted from an incorporeal space? The idea here is not that he is constrained to the earth. Rather, what is meant here is that his authority and place is removed by the advance of Christ. Let us keep in mind that this is symbolic. How can a spirit being that is not bound by our material world be restricted from the spiritual world? These questions give us insight to this dilemma of Satan's fall. It is not so much *where* he can go, but *what* he can do where he is found. The fall of Satan represents his judgment, his restricted reign and rule, which once was unfettered and free over the nations of this world. The same event will be covered again in the twelfth and the twentieth chapters, but from another perspective. What we are learning is that in this age the authority of Satan is curtailed, and as the kingdom of heaven advances, his authority is further diminished.

The fifth trumpet explains how in this age the Lord's glory and truth ebb, leading to a woeful plague of suffering on earth. Locusts are indicative of a plague of suffering that is remarkably hideous and tormenting, but not deadly. Much like the thirds afflicted by the revelation of the will of God in the seals, so the woes here are proportionate in scope and scale. During this present age, the Lord's trumpet is sounded, and with it, Satan is loosed to darken the glory of heaven and the wonders of God's word. And when that happens, suffering and torment prevail. A scorpion sting is not generally deadly, but it inflicts pain with poison. When Satan is loosed to open the pit of hell and work wonders in these last days, when he is loosed to slay the witnesses of our Lord on earth (The Lord's priestly and governmental witnesses which will be addressed later), the world is stricken, and great suffering follows.

That this torment comes from the bottomless pit tells us that it is often heresy and false teaching that it refers to in this text. Or it is the foolish traditions of men that rise to equality with God's word. That it only affects those that do not have the seal of the Lord on their foreheads tells us that only the non-elect are led to suffer the woes of error and false doctrines. That it is only for five months tells us that it is seasonal, that it is for a time, proportionate, and short-lived, as most errors arise, go away, only to recur later. The fact that the locusts have crowns, and the faces of men tells us that these are men of authority on earth, men of religion, majestically enthroned, leading masses to suffer at the hands of their error. The fact that they do not harm the vegetation tells us that this plague is isolated to the beliefs of men. Whenever in this age heresy and false doctrine arise, men suffer, heaven darkens, and woes follow the paths of these wretched creatures.

So pause and consider in sum what we have seen thus far in the trumpet blasts. They are woes, wherein the last three are far more woeful than the former four. The first four address the upsetting of governments, commerce, and the world's social orders, all of which is the Lord's doing, by which He brings judgment and conquest. These last three will be unique and more horrible for men, as they suffer for seasons, miserably, with little relief. Just as in the plagues of

Egypt the gods of Egypt were mocked, and Pharaoh was shown to be impotent and the Nile and its inhabitants were found suffering proportionate woes, so here we see that in this age when heresy abounds it is the loosing of Satan and the judgment of God upon this world. By this, the Lord brings judgment upon men. However, His own are kept safe; like Israel in Goshen, the true Israel of God does not suffer the deceits of Satan. They do not fall prey to the devil's lies neither are thy deluded by the darkening of heaven's truth. The fact that the king of these scorpions or false teachers is called Apollyon and Abaddon, the Greek and Hebrew for destroyer, shows us that Satan is the source of heresy and men are the creatures that are stung by his lies. He is loosed to destroy others along with them, but the Lord is the King that through these woes brings forth judgment and victory from heaven to earth.

The second woe follows and makes the first to seem minor compared to that which follows. For the second woe brings up the imagery of Babylon. Babylon, the great destroyer and judge of apostate Judah, who carried away the elect into a far-off land, is here seen in type. The fact that the angels of the river Euphrates are loosed to let the waters of the Euphrates flow proves this fact. For this is the river of life for Babylon. From the Euphrates Nebuchadnezzar arose to swiftly conquer and plunder the earth and the last tribe of Israel. The same imagery of horses and their armor recalls that of Habakkuk. Tied to the previous woe, this woe appears to bring the Lord's judgment upon the visible church, those stung by the Destroyer and his creatures, who were led to delusions from their hideous stings of doctrine. Now the Lord is seen to raise up a nation like unto Babylon, which is sent to judge and carry away those deceived.

The proof of this interpretation is found in verse 21, where it says,

> And the rest of the men which were not
> killed by these plagues yet repented not of the
> works of their hands, that they should not wor-
> ship devils, and idols of gold, and silver, and
> brass, and stone, and of wood: which neither can

see, nor hear, nor walk: Neither repented they of
their murders, nor of their sorceries, nor of their
fornication, nor of their thefts.

The visible apostate church is here in view. And as Judah was
the type of the apostate church of our day, so Babylon is said to slay
many and carry them away. Just like then where only a remnant of
Israel remained, so it will be in this age. We find then that the Lord
raises up ruthless kings to slay heretics and lead many away, captive
in their own deception in this age. What does this woe mean? It
means that in this age often the Lord judges the visible church at the
hands of earthly kings. As Babylon was the tool of the Lord's judgment for Judah, so are the nations like Babylon in this age employed
of the Lord to carry away the captive church in her error.

Chapter 10: An Interlude

One abiding truth and theme prevails throughout this revelation and that is the absolute sovereignty of God. Centered in Christ,
both in the previous age and in this the last age, the Lord's eternal
design, His decrees, and His active working have advanced to conquer this rebel and hostile world. It is the Lord that rides forth to
complete the eternal glorious conquest and redeeming purpose of the
Father. As the ninth chapter opens, one woe remains.

The first two woes were enough to strike terror in those observing the incomprehensible wonders of the Lord. It was He, the Lord,
who subverts and undermines the dragon's designs. Now, this last
woe shall be the compendium of the Lord's terror and glory. The
first four trumpets announced the waring advance of the kingdom of
heaven in conquering and subduing nations and governments, dis-
rupting their progress, undoing their schemes, and raising them up
and tearing them down at His discretion while all along leading those
not sealed by the Lord to their own delusions and imaginations, and
subsequently employing nations to undermine the subtle deception
of Satan within the visible church. History bears evidence of this
throughout, in fact, history is undeniable proof that the sovereign

Lord has orchestrated these events to the letter of Revelation. The Lord orchestrates all things to His glory while directing the world and its prince to their own demise. It is much like Haman in Esther, wherein the Lord employed the schemes and vitriol of the enemy of His people to that foe's own undoing. In this age, Satan and his allies and servants are constructing the gallows of their own doom while the Lord laughs in derision from heaven.

The last woe does not occur until the end of the eleventh chapter; that woe is short in scope, in that the victory of our Lord is announced. The ninth through eleventh chapters actually complete the sixth trumpet's announced woe. It is not a parenthesis. It is a continuation. The ninth chapter begins the second *aspect* of the sixth trumpet's announcement; the first part detailed the loosing of the Lord's judgment by raising up those like Babylon to judge the visible, apostate church, the second part will describe the Lord's care and deliverance of the invisible church. As is the case in each revelation, especial time and care is given to detail the Lord's oversight of the true Israel of God in this present age. Thus, chapter 9 is a pause in the details of the woe, a pause that allows the apostle to be emboldened and prepared for prophesying further and observing the remarkable sovereign design of the Lord with His elect.

An angel descends to announce the approach of the end of the Lord's glorious plan. He is titled a *mighty* angel. He has the appearance of one greater than an angel; for He has the covenant sign of the sovereign Lord over Him. He shines with the glory of the Almighty and His feet have the similar appearance of the Lamb's in chapter 1. Add to this the fact that He holds a small book in His hand, and it is clear that this is one like the Lord Himself. He is undeniably sovereign, as He stands upon the sea and the land. He roars like a lion. He speaks and thunders the seven thunders. This is a reflection of the Lamb Himself, the King of kings, the Lord Almighty. He is the One that has the scroll and the sovereignty to stay time, as He announces that "there should be time no longer" and "the mystery of God should be finished." It is He in the reflection of this angel that appears on earth to stand and orchestrate what follows. Each revelation ends with the day of the Lord, Christ's return, the end of all things. This sixth trumpet mirrors that fact, just like the sixth seal, and now John is prepared to see the advancing glory of the Lord in conquest to the end.

A caution is given to John and the reader. For the seven thunders that echo the Lion's roar remind us that we are but finite creatures. Though we have been given knowledge, great knowledge through this book, and though this book is an unveiling of the eternal design, still we are limited in our understanding of the scope and order of the divine will. Even now, beholding all we have seen with John, we know so little of the divine agency. We see a grand view of His glorious will. We behold a glorious tapestry of His sovereign work, but even then, much we do not understand, much we still do not know. Thus, that which the seven thunders echo (like the twenty-ninth Psalm echoes the seven aspects of the sovereign glory of the Lord) are yet sealed and kept from us. It is God that we do not fully know. He is incomprehensible. He is immense. He is above all. As Hendriksen says, "There are other forces at work; there are other principles that are operating in this universe, namely, the seven thunders. What they are we do not know" (124). This timely appearance of the angel that precedes the final revelation of the Lord's care and deliverance of His beloved reminds John he is not done, reminds us that we are feeble creatures that know so little of the Lord's sovereign glory, and reminds us all that the Lord sovereignly governs and orchestrates the eternal purpose of His will in creation, and His will is impeccable and glorious, too glorious to behold. The mighty angel that appears and thunders is the same that ushers in the end, but that end is veiled in glory.

It is here that John, like Ezekiel and Jeremiah before him, is led to act out a parable for the reader. He is commanded to take and eat the little scroll, little most likely because so much has already been made known, a scroll because it is the sovereign decrees of the Lord. This is what John is to prophecy, and that which he shall prophecy is what the Lord has planned, and it is as always bittersweet; sweet in wonder and marvel for the awe of the covenanting Lord, and bitter in the means by which the Lord brings judgment. John's work is not done; he would leave Patmos. He would write. That which was revealed to him was to be prophesied "again before many peoples, and nations, and tongues, and kings." How sad that for so long this book has been kept upon the shelf. How sad that so few have taken to unlocking this book's mysteries. This book is vital to the life of the church until the end of this age. It contains knowledge of the grand scheme of the Lord in this the second of ages to complete His glorious plan. It provides courage and confidence to the elect that they will not be forsaken. It provides certainty to this hostile world that their end is imminent and certain. Away with those that would make this book a fairytale of some future time; this book is for now! It is to be digested just as it was by John, that we might muse in the Lord's glory and taste of the bitterness of His majestic fury. Chapter 10 is the prelude to the end. It is a pause to remind all that our holy Lord is sovereign.

Chapter 11: The Final Conquest

Chapter 11 begins with the continuation of the tenth chapter's interlude, which is, in fact, but a continuation of the sixth trumpet; the two parts being this, first, those not sealed unto the Lord that are led down the path of idolatry and sorceries fail to repent of their deeds, and the second, the readying of the elect for the end of days. This is the same pattern observed in all three sections of this spoken of as *after these things*. The visible church is judged while the true church is delivered. Thus, as the eleventh chapter begins, the accounting of the habitation of God among men is ordered. Drawing upon the Babylonian prophesies of old, John, like Ezekiel, is ordered to measure the temple of God. Its similarities to Ezekiel's measurements are telling, but not exact, as now the fullness of time and revelation of things hidden are now revealed. Now can be measured the full abiding place of the Lord. Ezekiel's measurement was dwarfed in comparison to John's, just as Ezekiel's prophecy dwarfed in the knowledge of the full design of the Lord.

Yet upon measuring, John is given a restriction to his measurement; he is not to measure the apostate part of the visible temple. We also see that this measurement is not yet complete, as there remains a time before it is complete. Drawing upon the recurring measurement of time, which is at times measured in months, days, or years, it is here drawn out as forty-two months, demonstrating the brevity of time remaining. However, that same time is measured in days when it refers to the two witnesses of the Lord within the temple. What is brief for the world's approaching day of judgment is elongated when viewed from the suffering of the true people of the Lord.

The temple is the church, the court of the Gentiles is the visible church, and the two witnesses are the magisterial and priestly roles of the true church on earth. These two witnesses were identified in Zechariah four as represented by Joshua and Zerubbabel. Joshua, the high priest of the returned remnant and Zerubbabel the representative of the abiding kingly line of Judah. Ramsey says,

> A further examination of the context shows that these two anointed ones, or sons of oil, were the two great offices through which God's power and grace flowed into the church, and sustained its light, the priestly and kingly, the functions of which were then exercised by Joshua and Zerubbabel, who are here addressed the name as the chosen instruments by whom God would establish the theocracy. These two offices, indeed, are so essentially connected with the church's life, that they always have been, and always must be, the sole means through which it receives the divine influences. (472)

What is seen by John is that amidst the advance of days in this age there will arise days where the invisible church of the Lord shall appear to be vanquished and subdued, almost to her extinction on earth, where it is as if the priestly and kingly roles of the true Israel on earth shall be slain. However, there shall be days of reformation, there shall be times where she shall arise from the dust and ashes to prophesy of the Lord once more. We see that the beast, that nation arisen from the gates of hell, is imbued of the devil with fury and bloodshed, as he goes forth to make war with the true Israel of God. When he succeeds it is in the visible church that the remnants of the Lord's true church on earth will remain. Thus, it says, "Their dead bodies shall lie in the street of the great city, which spiritually is called Sodom and Egypt, where also our Lord was crucified." This is the visible church, likened unto Israel of old, within which often the apostasy is so great that the vestiges of the true church are all that remain in her midst. So it is that she is as dead in her midst. There is perhaps no more perfect illustration of this then the late Middle Ages, where the visible church in the west was apostate, and seemingly, the true church forever lay dead. Yet from the midst of that great lamb-like beast there arose she that was once as dead, rising from her very midst in the days of the Reformation, coming to life again. This is the second woe. Put in the scope of three and a half days, it is but a moment that the truth appeared eclipsed.

What is remarkable is the great joy that the world takes in our demise. Regardless of her futility, the world pursues her own end with a vengeance. The Lord's own are a torment to this world. Our mere presence infuriates the dragon, the beast, the false prophet, the Whore, and all those who do not have the seal of the living God. And while they yet see the power of God raise up from the ashes, as His glory is found residing in His true church, as this world and its kingdoms are judged, still they repent not of their deeds. In fact, the world will but try to duplicate the Lord's glory at all costs, only to fail. This chapter fits so well the events of history itself up until the time of the Reformation, yet we must remember that these visions are not chronological nor successive but mere allusions to the events of this age. This has happened, perhaps often, and shall happen again. We also must remember that this is the sixth trumpet, the second of three great woes for the earth, whose end is not yet.

As chapter 11 continues, the third woe and final trumpet is prepared to sound. It is noted that the angel indicates that the final trumpet *cometh quickly.* This indicates once more that the end is sudden. Each and every successive revelation in this age approaches the end with the same abruptness, as the close of this age is certain to arrive in this fashion. When the end arrives, it will arrive without warning, it will be succinct, and it will not linger. It will simply come with this declaration, that "the kingdoms of this world are become the kingdoms of our Lord, and of his Christ; and he shall reign for ever and ever."

This is the goal of this age, this is the design and purpose of God from the beginning, that as this age approaches its end, He will be found to reign victorious. Christ is seen overcoming once and for all the kingdoms of this world. Thus, the trumpets represent the view in Revelation of the Lord making war against the kingdoms of this world, and as the end approaches, His completion of that conquest. It is said, "And the nations were angry, and thy wrath is come, and the time of the dead, that they should be judged, and that thou shouldest give reward unto thy servants the prophets, and to the saints, and them that fear thy name, small and great; and shouldest destroy them which destroy the earth." As the seals ended with silence, so the trumpets end with equal finality. The Lord is found victorious, the battle is won, and the He executes His wrath and vengeance in a moment. It is no long and drawn-out final engagement, it is no great battle leading to victory; instead, as the end comes, it arrives with but a final declaration. The Lord finishes this age with a trumpet blast.

The last woe is judgment. The final trumpet blast is the end. There is no further threat to the throne, there is no remaining enemy to subdue, the end comes, and judgment is declared. We find that the consequence of the final trumpet blast is the eternal reign of our Lord, and our reign with Him. Seeing the twenty-four elders fall before Him to give honor and glory reminds the reader of the full and final culmination of this blast. The church is complete. The elect are fully accounted for. The enemies are laid low. There are the spoils of war, as "the kingdoms of this world are the kingdoms of our Lord and of His Christ." There is the adjudication of the prisoners, as "Thy wrath is come, and the time of the dead, that they should be judged, and that thou shouldest give reward unto thy servants the prophets, and to the saints, and them that fear thy name, small and great; and shouldest destroy them which destroy the earth." The final view is of the completed house of God, the summation of His work, the temple built, every stone placed, as the Lord's are His and He will abide with them forever. As the seventh trumpet ends, "And the temple of God was opened in heaven, and there was seen in his temple the ark of his testament: and there were lightnings, and voices, and thunderings, and an earthquake, and great hail," we are reminded of what this was truly all about; His glory, His justice, His conquest, our salvation, all that we might reign and abide with Him forever. As it finishes, we are found complete in Him. He has finished His work, and it is glorious.

CHAPTERS 12–22

AN OVERVIEW OF THE LORD'S WRATH AND JUDGMENT

The last portion of Revelation, this final view, looks to the defeat and conquest of the Lord's enemies. From the nations of this world figured in a Beast, the allurements of this world shown in the Great Whore, and Satan himself, the devil, the chief and first adversary of our Lord. While the coming of Christ and His work on the cross and defeat of death in the resurrection did much to wound and restrict the devil, still his ultimate demise is advancing and forthcoming. We must realize that these chapters that remain teach us that God's wrath is presently being poured out upon our enemies and will one day be complete. One might say this is the age of God's wrath, fully explaining what Paul meant when he said in Romans 1:18, "For the wrath of God is revealed from heaven against all ungodliness and unrighteousness of men, who hold the truth in unrighteousness." This is the already yet not yet tension of Revelation; we hear that the Lord "hath made us kings and priests unto God and his Father," which is now and fully yet to be realized, so it is with the wrath of God, which is presently being displayed against all ungodliness and unrighteousness but shall soon be complete. The final section of Revelation shows us the glorious and righteous judgment of God against all our foes and the certain glory that awaits us as the bride of Christ.

Chapter 12: The War's Reinvigoration and Final Days

This chapter begins the third and final revelation of this present age. The first view portrayed in a sealed book was of the divine decrees, that eternally predestined by the Lord for this world's judgment and His people's salvation. The second view introduced by trumpets was of the warfare made by the Lord against this rebellious world, showing His engagement and success unto victory over all kingdoms, principalities, and powers, until the kingdoms of this world were made the kingdoms of our Lord. Now comes the final view set in the likeness of bowls poured out, from which we shall see that all enemies of the Lord shall be put asunder. This section shall show that this age is the age of judgment and wrath, wherein the Lord executes His vengeance against all enemies from the first to the last. For the chief enemy and adversary remains, Satan, who while greatly hindered and routed, he who was the instrumental cause of our misery, who along with all his allies yet remains to be subdued. As John and the church in his day struggled and wrestled with this foe and his forces, here is given a final glance at his certain demise and our sure salvation.

A third and final rewind begins this third revelation of this which *shall shortly come to pass.* Twice before in both the fourth and eighth chapter, John was given to behold the events at the start of this age. The scroll was given to our Lord "who hath prevailed to open the book, and to loose the seven seals thereof" (Rev. 5:5). It was upon the ascension and enthronement of our Lord again that that revealed in the sealed scroll was made known. So it was in the preparation for the sounding of the trumpets. When it was said that "there fell a great star from heaven, burning as it were a lamp, and it fell upon the third part of the rivers, and upon the fountains of waters" (Rev. 8:10), it was the ascension of Christ in glory that led to Satan's downfall at the start of this age. So here once more, as the twelfth chapter opens, we rewind the clock again back to the start of this age, but yet a bit before, to that moment just before the incarnation of our Christ, where it says, "And she being with child cried, travailing in birth, and pained to be delivered" (Rev. 12:2). Each of the three views of this age, referred to as "the things which shall shortly come to pass" begin with the success of the Lord in the first advent.

So with John, we the reader are taken back to the beginning once more, back to the start of this age, and as before, it begins with the coming of our Christ. Recall that Revelation 4–22 is bookended by these two events, the first and second coming of our Lord, the events of His incarnation and His glorious return. Here, drawing upon the dream of Joseph in Genesis 37, we are shown a similar vision of Israel, of "a woman clothed with the sun, and the moon under her feet, and upon her head a crown of twelve stars." What Joseph saw in his dream was similarly of "the sun and the moon and the eleven stars made obeisance to me" (Gen. 37:9), and what John saw was like unto it, where the woman is Israel and she is of full and ripe age, poised to give birth. While Hendriksen calls this woman the church, "That woman symbolizes the Church (cf. Is. 50: 1; 54: 1; Ho. 2: 1; Eph. 5: 32). Scripture emphasizes the fact that the Church in both dispensations is one" (135), and he is correct, still the broader view here is Israel, true Israel, which is the church, the woman, the bride of Christ, who is His betrothed.

Central to understanding this chapter and the entirety of the book itself is understanding the identity of Israel. All Israel is she that is comprised of all the elect of God, in the past age principally made up of Abraham's descendants in the flesh, but now comprised of both Jew and Gentile. Thus, when in Romans 11 Paul says, "All Israel shall be saved," he is speaking of the truly elect. Israel, both Jew and Gentile, those of faith alone, are those as we saw before identified as "the hundred and forty and four thousand of all the tribes of the children of Israel," comprised of a great multitude, "which no man could number, of all nations, and kindreds, and people, and tongues." Here I would prefer to call this woman in Revelation 12:1 Israel and not the church, mainly because the church is a narrower view of the concept of the elect. Israel refers to all those of the faith of Abraham, of those called out by grace alone, and while Israel represents the covenant people of God from start to finish, from Adam to the last, she is indicative of her that is the betrothed of the Lord, bound to Him from everlasting. She is the one that wrested with the

Lord and prevailed. She is the one from which the Christ came forth, as we read in Matthew, "The book of the generation of Jesus Christ, the son of David, the son of Abraham." Therefore, the woman of Revelation 12:1 is not Mary, but that foreshadowed in Joseph's dream. Remember that all is symbolic, thus this is no mere woman.

We find that the third vision begins with the days preceding the incarnation. Those days are likened to the days of Moses, where once the prince of this world, Pharaoh, stood to devour the deliverer. So here, another prince of this world, Herod, stands to devour the coming Deliverer. But Herod is not the one in view here; here we see he that is behind those men, it is he called the dragon, "that old serpent, called the Devil, and Satan, which deceiveth the whole world." He that begins this age opposed to the redemptive, eternal plan of God is Satan, who always has sought to impede God's glorious redemption. He that began this age seeking to stop the Redeemer's advent shall end this age judged for that opposition. This third view here of this age is that shown of the vantage of the Lord's judgment, judgment to the chief adversary of our God and of His Christ, and judgment to all those allied with him and opposed to the Almighty hand of God.

The introduction of Satan with all his various names and manifestations tells us that a broad overview is here found. He that has since the beginning endeavored to stay the hand of God shall in this age be fully and finally judged. The dragon in chapter 12 begins much as Haman began in Esther's day, certain he would prevail, poised to once and for all slay all those of the Lord's favor. In Esther, Haman was such a type, as we saw that "Haman saw that Mordecai bowed not, nor did him reverence, then was Haman full of wrath. And he thought scorn to lay hands on Mordecai alone; for they had shewed him the people of Mordecai: wherefore Haman sought to destroy all the Jews that were throughout the whole kingdom of Ahasuerus, even the people of Mordecai" (Esther 3:5f), and just as Haman's fury and wrath and every contrivance sought the end of the Lord and His children without success, so will Satan and his allies find no lasting success. In this age they are finding themselves judged. This age began with the dragon poised once more to subvert and impede the Lord's designed redemptive plan.

Time and again Satan has stood to impede the Lord's glory. With the fall of Adam, he sought to plunge this race into lasting damnation and rebellion, but the Lord provided a promise, saying, "I will put enmity between thee and the woman, and between thy seed and her seed; it shall bruise thy head, and thou shalt bruise his heel" (Gen. 3:15). With the death of Abel, once more the dragon presumed success, but we find, "Adam knew his wife again; and she bare a son, and called his name Seth: For God, said she, hath appointed me another seed instead of Abel, whom Cain slew," and so it was once again that the promise remained. Then there were the days of Judah, Er and Onan slain by the Lord, one for wickedness, another for refusing to participate in the propagation of that seed, so that Tamar was to be kept from the last son of Judah, as Judah said, "Lest peradventure he die also, as his brethren did. And Tamar went and dwelt in her father's house." Ah, but the Lord had a plan, and through the unrighteous acts of Judah we read of twins born to Tamar, so that the Lord's promise might break through again, as we read of the twins' birth, "And it came to pass, as he drew back his hand, that, behold, his brother came out: and she said, How hast thou broken forth? this breach be upon thee: therefore his name was called Pharez." How often the dragon stood in the way, seeking to stay the hand of God, only to find the Lord provide a seed, to breach through the impasse, and to make a way to our salvation and His glory.

So once more, as Christ was to be born, we find that old dragon once more was found standing "before the woman which was ready to be delivered, for to devour her child as soon as it was born," and once more we find that he will not prevail. Now comes the final act of this great warfare. Now comes the end of this long battle. Now comes Satan's judgment, and with him all those allied with him. What starts here in chapter 12 will not end until the final chapter. It will span this age from the coming of Christ, which was a breach in this age until His return, the dragon will seek to once and for all provide an impasse to the Lord's redemptive plan, but he will not succeed. For we find that his days are short and his doom certain. What a blessed prize this was for John and the saints of his day to behold. All their adversaries would be ruined. All their foes would be defeated. Despite every evidence to the contrary, they were not winning and would not succeed to impede the Lord's glory and promised redemption. They are yet under the wrath of almighty God.

When we see the dragon in chapter 12, he is described *as having seven heads and ten horns, and seven crowns upon his heads.* This symbolic representation of Satan as ruling the nations of this world shows us that he stands behind the powers of this world. While in John's day, it was principally Rome that was in view, and its dominion is undoubtedly pictured here in the imagery of seven heads and ten horns, still the image had broader import. For it refers to all the nations of this world throughout this age that are at the beckon of the devil. There is no such thing as a Christian nation. Every attempt to define one as such fails and is contrary to scripture. Revelation shows us that the nations of this age throughout this world are under the oversight of Satan. He is as Paul says, "the prince of the power of the air." They are all under his dominion, and while that dominion is curtailed and receding in this age, they still remain under his charge. Rome is but one example of an empire under the oversight of Satan. While under the general providence of our Lord the Lord sovereignly appoints the course and rule of these nations, still they remain under the dominion of the evil one. This here then is symbolic of such dominion.

Satan brings with him a host of demons, as pictured in his tail that "drew the third part of the stars of heaven, and did cast them to the earth." Great agency and alliances formed to unite against the coming of Christ and continue to seek to stand in His way. The fact that the dragon stood before the woman reminds us that Herod was his servant. He told the wise men of Chaldea, "Go and search diligently for the young child; and when ye have found him, bring me word again, that I may come and worship him also," but only in pretense, as he sought to slay him. As we find later, "When Herod, when he saw that he was mocked of the wise men, was exceeding wroth, and sent forth, and slew all the children that were in Bethlehem, and in all the coasts thereof, from two years old and under, according to the time which he had diligently inquired of the wise men" (Matt. 2:16f), this was the dragon, instrumental through the agencies of men and nations, seeking to impede the Lord's redemptive glory, but without success. Revelation 12 opens with the forces of this world poised once more to begin this age opposed to the glorious work of our Lord.

John next is shown that which underlies this whole final act, summed up in these words, "She brought forth a man child, who was to rule all nations with a rod of iron: and her child was caught up unto God, and to his throne. And the woman fled into the wilderness, where she hath a place prepared of God, that they should feed her there a thousand two hundred and threescore days." Christ ascended victorious to rule as it says, *all nations*, which ends this first drama. The woman's final days are drawn out not in years, or months, but in days, signifying her time of flight is short. But here begins the import of this final vision, the judgment of the dragon and all his allies. For from the start of this chapter, where we read, "There appeared a great wonder in heaven," unto the end, where we read, "And the devil that deceived them was cast into the lake of fire and brimstone, where the beast and the false prophet are, and shall be tormented day and night for ever and ever," we shall behold the pouring out of God's wrath and judgment in this age against our foes. The intent of this final revelation is to show the judgment and execution of God's wrath upon all our foes, so begins the dragon's judgment.

With each successive event in this final vision, Satan's dominion and liberty shall be shown to be curtailed. Recall that these are not sequential actions but various ways in which God's judgment proceeds. When Christ appeared, the dragon's end drew near. When Christ ascended, his liberty was rescinded. We find the devil's judgment begins with the ascension of the Lord, as he that once held sway over the nations finds it lost, when we read, "She brought forth a man child, who was to rule all nations with a rod of iron: and her child was caught up unto God, and to his throne." Thus begins his judgment, for Christ is to "rule all nations with a rod of iron." When Christ ascended,

> [t]here was war in heaven: Michael and his
> angels fought against the dragon; and the dragon

fought and his angels, And prevailed not; neither was their place found any more in heaven. And the great dragon was cast out, that old serpent, called the Devil, and Satan, which deceiveth the whole world: he was cast out into the earth, and his angels were cast out with him.

This is what Christ spoke of when He said, "I beheld Satan as lightning fall from heaven" (Luke 10:18); as our Lord's dominion grows, so Satan's is curtailed.

This is the age of the beginning of the end for the devil and his allies. With the coming and ascension of our Lord came the end to our adversaries' accusations in heaven. The foolish error of many that imagine a prior time of Satan's being cast out of heaven is but a myth. One such passage used to try and prove that long before the incarnation of Christ Satan fell is Isaiah 14. There, the passage is improperly exegeted. As Calvin says of Isaiah 14:12,

> The exposition of this passage, which some have given, as if it referred to Satan, has arisen from ignorance; for the context plainly shows that these statements must be understood in reference to the king of the Babylonians. But when passages of Scripture are taken up at random, and no attention is paid to the context, we need not wonder that mistakes of this kind frequently arise. Yet it was an instance of very gross ignorance, to imagine that Lucifer was the king of devils, and that the Prophet gave him this name. But as these inventions have no probability whatever, let us pass by them as useless fables. (Commentaries Isaiah)

Here in this age has the true judgment and wrath against our foe begun.

It cannot be imagined that there was actual *war* in heaven, in the sense of armies, weapons, and strife, but here the imagery draws upon such concepts, that we might come to see that it was with great conquest that Christ ascended, having proven victorious at the cross. He was vindicated in the resurrection. From there our Lord ascended to His throne to drive out the dragon from the heavens. With Him seated it is as if every accusation against us has ceased. Now He is our mediator, our advocate and High Priest, who has put to rest the accusations against us. The picture here is that he that once deceived and lied is judged, judged and driven out to no more deceive the nations. Before Christ came, the world was chained in darkness. It was under the sway and dominion of the evil one, who deceived the whole world. But through the victory of Christ in His first work Satan's reign and dominion are curtailed. Now Christ is said to "rule all nations with a rod of iron." And now was begun the beginning of the end of his rebellion.

With these words the final revelation is summed up,

> Now is come salvation, and strength, and the kingdom of our God, and the power of his Christ: for the accuser of our brethren is cast down, which accused them before our God day and night. And they overcame him by the blood of the Lamb, and by the word of their testimony; and they loved not their lives unto the death. Therefore rejoice, ye heavens, and ye that dwell in them. Woe to the inhabiters of the earth and of the sea! for the devil is come down unto you, having great wrath, because he knoweth that he hath but a short time.

From this declaration, the revelation of judgment and salvation commences. Here will be the full and final assessment of the Lord's design in this age, to judge the dragon and his allies and to deliver His bride unto the end.

The final verses of chapter 12 sum up all that follows, serving as a precursory analysis of the events that follow. What follows will be, "The dragon, seeing, that he was cast unto the earth, he persecuted the woman which brought forth the man child." The woman will be persecuted, but in the end, she will be delivered. The dragon will pursue her but never succeed in her ruin, as we read, "The woman were given two wings of a great eagle, that she might fly into the wilderness, into her place, where she is nourished for a time, and times, and half a time, from the face of the serpent." Once more the time is given as certain but undefined, but with this designation of *time* it is left a bit ambiguous. Nevertheless, her flight is protected. With this we can expect in the chapters to follow the woman's flight, but also the devil's wroth, as we read,

> And the serpent cast out of his mouth water as a flood after the woman, that he might cause her to be carried away of the flood. And the earth helped the woman, and the earth opened her mouth, and swallowed up the flood which the dragon cast out of his mouth. And the dragon was wroth with the woman, and went to make war with the remnant of her seed, which keep the commandments of God, and have the testimony of Jesus Christ.

This is what we shall find indicative of this age, the age of judgment and wrath, the age of care and salvation, during which the dragon, our old foe, and our Lord's, shall be once and for all subdued, he and all his allies.

Chapter 13: Judging the Beast

The previous chapter ended with this declaration: "The dragon was wroth with the woman, and went to make war with the remnant of her seed, which keep the commandments of God, and have the testimony of Jesus Christ." Now begins the final thrust of Satan in his futile efforts that remain. This verse indicates the nature of this age; Satan is enraged. His time is short, and with great futility and despair he goes to make war despite his certain ruin. His judgment is begun and is heretofore to be completed. The stage being set for this final conflict, now begins the explication of that remaining effort of the dragon to prevent what is certainly inevitable now. This last act of war shall culminate with the Lord's victory and the dragon's judgment, but until that day hostilities continue, as even now the Lord's wrath is being poured out upon His enemies until that day. As warfare ensues, John is said to be standing *upon the sand of the sea.* Whether this is literal or not (as John is on the island of Patmos), the point is that John is set to watch and behold as the battle of this final age begins, and it begins in the sea.

From the sea, the beast is said to rise. We remember that the basic design of Revelation is symbolic and therefore conclude that this is not intended as literal; instead, from this vantage John will observe the rising of the world's empires and nations of this age as the stage is set for the final war. It all begins at the sea, the sea of humanity. The sea in scripture is often employed symbolically as representing the hostile mass of fallen humanity. Hendriksen says, "The sea represents nations and their governments (cf. Is. 17: 12), where the roaring of peoples is compared to the roaring of the sea; and the surging of nations to the surging of mighty waters" (p. 145). Isaiah uses the likeness of a sea to represent the tumultuous rebels brought to judge Israel, as Isaiah said,

> Woe to the multitude of many people,
> which make a noise like the noise of the seas; and
> to the rushing of nations, that make a rushing
> like the rushing of mighty waters! The nations
> shall rush like the rushing of many waters: but
> God shall rebuke them, and they shall flee far off,
> and shall be chased as the chaff of the mountains
> before the wind, and like a rolling thing before
> the whirlwind. (Isa. 17:12f)

What is detailed here is not new. The same imagery appears in Daniel 7, from which the beasts of Daniel arose from the sea. There, the beasts were seen as representing the intertestamental nations of Babylon, Persia, Greece, and Rome. They were said to be as a lion, a bear, a leopard, and another called merely dreadful and terrible. What John is shown is quite like that which Daniel saw, yet it is different.

Here the beast that arises is comprised of all four aspects of the beasts of Daniel. Clearly, this is not one nation, but that which represents the nations of this age which arise from the sea of the hostile agency of fallen men, arisen to exercise dominion and authority, per the providence of Almighty God, to the end of making war with the God of heaven and earth. The reason why this beast is composed of all those characteristics of the previous four beasts of Daniel is twofold, first, the beast here introduced is vastly superior to those others, and second, this beast is representative of all nations and empires that arise during the scope of these last days. This is not one nation. What is remarkable about the appearance of the beast of Revelation 13 is the similarity of this beast to Rome. The description of the beast having "seven heads and ten horns, and upon his horns ten crowns, and upon his heads the name of blasphemy," conjures up in the mind Rome and its historic description. In one sense this is Rome, but it is more than Rome. Rome is but the beginning of beasts that are represented by the beast of Revelation 13.

The best evidence for this interpretation is Revelation itself, as chapter 17 contains the explication of this chapter. There an angel explains to John the meaning of the beast and sea. The angel describes the beast as it which *was, and is not*; therefore, this is not one nation in time, but the nations of this age over time, likened unto all the beasts of Daniel now consolidated in the empires of this age. This is the beast of the age, which arises time and again in various forms and fashions throughout these last days. It is and is not and shall be yet again. Further, it is raised up by the instigation of the dragon, as it says, "It shall ascend out of the bottomless pit, and go into perdition." In this chapter, it is noted, "the dragon gave him his power, and his seat, and great authority." As was said, this beast is but the manifestation of the fury and futility of the dragon, who seeks to make war with God and His elect. Thus, it says, "These shall make war with the Lamb, and the Lamb shall overcome them: for he is Lord of lords, and King of kings: and they that are with him are called, and chosen, and faithful" (17:14). Scripture is always the best means of interpreting scripture. We need not guess as to the nature of the revelation of chapter 13, for it is explained later.

The most profound part of this image is found in these words:

> And they worshipped the dragon which gave power unto the beast: and they worshipped the beast, saying, Who is like unto the beast? who is able to make war with him? And there was given unto him a mouth speaking great things and blasphemies; and power was given unto him to continue forty and two months. And he opened his mouth in blasphemy against God, to blaspheme his name, and his tabernacle, and them that dwell in heaven.

We find in this chapter that it is the goal of our adversary to claim the glory of the Lord as his own. His ultimate aim is blaspheming the true God. Thus, he is said to mimic God and seek His glory.

Peculiarly, we read that the beast is wounded, "One of his heads as it were wounded to death; and his deadly wound was healed: and all the world wondered after the beast." Like the magicians of Pharaoh's court, the devil's own are ever seeking to mimic the glory of the Lord and His works. We should not be surprised when the world seeks to duplicate what the Lord has done. Kings, emperors, rulers, and tyrants, have time and again sought the honor of God. Nebuchadnezzar dared boast, taking the Lord's glory as his own. Here we find that the dragon's goal is to mimic the glories of the Lord and His own, for just as the two witnesses of the Lord were miraculously raised from the seeming dead, so here the beast apes the Lord. The goal of the dragon in this age is to employ men in the pursuit of the Lord's glory, by way of sorcery and magic, just as Jannes and Jambres withstood Moses, so the dragon and his beast seeks to imitate the Lord. The blasphemous nature of verses 4–6 in this thirteenth chapter show us just how hideous are the forces of this world.

This first part of chapter 13 makes it clear that in this age nations, kingdoms, and empires shall be compelled by the dragon to rise up and make war with the woman. His goal is blasphemy, that he might rob the Lord of His glory. This world, its masses, its nations and kings, its empires, and rulers, are all employed by hell itself in these days to blaspheme our God. But our Lord is sovereign and we, like John, are reminded of this when we read,

> And it was given unto him to make war with the saints, and to overcome them: and power was given him over all kindreds, and tongues, and nations. And all that dwell upon the earth shall worship him, whose names are not written in the book of life of the Lamb slain from the foundation of the world. If any man have an ear, let him hear. He that leadeth into captivity shall go into captivity: he that killeth with the sword must be killed with the sword. Here is the patience and the faith of the saints.

This age is the age of warfare. The goal of the world, its kingdoms, and its ruler is to subdue us and blaspheme our God. We cannot be deceived; the world is not our friend. We are not to seek allegiances and commonalities with them. We are not to be in fellowship with Belial. He is our foe. The nations of this world are allied against us and our King. The peoples of this world are employed of the dragon to give him the glory and serve the beast. There is not a nation on earth that does not belong to this unholy alliance; all nations are risen from the cursed masses and energized by the devil himself.

These are the last days. Having begun with a beast of great wonder, Rome, that was unlike any other in majesty, glory, wealth, and power, she has been worshipped throughout this age. Many others have sought to emulate her. And while there have been nations that have appeared welcoming to the church, none have been or shall be our friend. The nations of this world are in allegiance with Satan, they are risen from the pit of hell, and their goal is to blaspheme our God. Ours is a plight. Ours is a flight. As we read, "Here is the patience and the faith of the saints." Everyone around us, both within and without the visible church, are in allegiance with the devil. They are part and parcel of the nations and kingdoms of this world, whose goal and design, is to blaspheme our God and seek our demise. Is it any wonder ours is a difficult pilgrimage? It is clear to see how errant men have been, how they have been misled to seek alliances with this world. Time and again throughout these last days the church has sought partnerships with nations. The visible church has often considered this world her friend. Yet in this age, apart from the elect, there is no person, nation, or dominion that is not subjugated to the pit of hell. We are at war. Our Lord is conquering this world. Our time is short, and as it says in verse 9, "If any man have an ear, let him hear." This is the age of kingdoms in conflict. It is the age of the Lamb advancing His glory. It is the age of conquest, conquest of the dragon and his dominion. It is the age of wrath, it is the age of fury and futility, it is the age to end all ages. Let us not be deceived; this world, its kingdoms, and its inhabitants are not our friends.

An interesting thought is found in Hendriksen, where he notes, "This beast assumes different forms; it has seven heads. Now it is Old Babylonia; then Assyria; next, New Babylonia; Medo-Persia; Macedonia; Rome, etc. But though the forms differ, the essence remains the same: worldly government directed against the Church" (146). This thought lends to the idea of the succession of nations. Beginning with Daniel's four kingdoms, added to this is that old nation of Babel, then Assyria, this leaves a seventh, which is indicative of all kingdoms of both ages. Simply put, if we begin with Babel in Genesis, add to it Assyria, and then the four nations of Daniel, one final Beast remains; that beast is this final beast. Yet it is not a literal nation. Instead, it is the Beast, which represents the nature of all nations in this age. It is found containing all the aspects of those of the past.

This interpretation indicates to us that in this age the dragon is employing all the principals of those old nations along with the empires and kingdoms of this age in one final attempt to subdue the Lord. We can deduce then that this beast in Revelation 13 is not a singular nation, but the whole of all nations in this age that comprise the worldly governments that are allied against our Lord and His church. Caution is warranted for all in their reading of Revelation. We err when we seek to give meaning to the symbols of Revelation with any singular situation or occurrence in this age. In this last section of Revelation, the Lord employs *concepts* that are evident in this age; what is revealed is not a blueprint of history. It is not as Daniel. Therefore, Hendriksen's association of this beast with the seven beasts of history is accurate; the first six are past, the last is now; this age the beast is seen as one, one representing every manifestation of empires and nations in these last days, which employ all worldly power to blaspheme and denounce our Lord and His beloved.

The vision continues with the rise of a second beast. It is similar to the first, but this time is seen bearing the semblance of the Lamb. The consummate example of this lamblike Beast in history is the Holy Roman Empire. As the Roman Empire fell, being overrun by the Barbarians, only to give rise to another empire like unto the first, but this time wed with the church, here is this example in John's purview. When worldly nations and empires unite with the visible church, we find this lamblike Beast. In this age, not only are empires and kingdoms created by the designs of the dragon bearing a secular form, idolatrous, and bloodthirsty, but at times, they arise with the semblance of the church. There is no denying that what John is shown is uncannily similar to Western history; Rome, the beast arose bearing the construct mentioned, with "seven heads and ten horns, and upon his horns ten crowns, and upon his heads the name of blasphemy," and after its fall it seemingly resurrected in the days of Charlemagne, when Pope Leo III crowned Charlemagne emperor. However, the designation in the seventeenth chapter of this beast's reign as *was, and is not,* tells us that Rome and the Holy Roman Empire are but an example of that foretold in this chapter. This age will and has seen this occur and it shall occur again. Nations rise to blaspheme our God. Often, they arise united with the visible church.

The fact that this is a beast tells us that it is an empire or nation similar to the previous beast arisen to oppose our Lord; however, that this one comes from the land rather than the sea indicates that it is from the existing social and governmental structures that are in existence. The two horns speak to power and this beast bears two, one for the civil authority it exercises, and one for the ecclesiastical authority it exercises. This beast while similar to the first, is wholly different. It is the false prophet, it is of antichrist, it is he that derives his power from the dragon but looks like the lamb. Its goal is to mimic the glory and power of God. So like the Lamb that arose to glory, this lamblike beast employs the resurrection of the previous beast to obtain the worship due to the true Lamb. This is the apostate church bearing the power of the nations, whose goal is to blaspheme God and obtain the worship of men for itself. We read he,

> Causeth the earth and them which dwell therein to worship the first beast, whose deadly wound was healed. And he doeth great wonders, so that he maketh fire come down from heaven on the earth in the sight of men, And deceiveth them that dwell on the earth by the means of those miracles which he had power to do in the sight of the beast; saying to them that dwell on the earth, that they should make an image to the beast, which had the wound by a sword, and did live.

Like Jannes and Jambres the dragon employs the two horned beast to seduce the world. The goal of the dragon is to rob God of His glory. In this age the dragon is working to this end.

We see then that the thirteenth chapter is a broad overview of this age and the dragon's designs in it. He seeks to blaspheme the Lord and bring the world to worship him. He employs the empires and nations of this world to this end. He mimics the work and wonders of our God. He brings beasts wed with the likeness of a lamb to draw the world to his worship, all to this end, that they might be marked as his, as we read, "And he causeth all, both small and great, rich and poor, free and bond, to receive a mark in their right hand, or in their foreheads." Here the alliance begins; the dragon, the beast, the beast like a lamb, and all those that receive the mark of the beast. The empires and kingdoms of this world, the wedded empires and nations comprised of ecclesiastical authority, along with all those not chosen of God, are in this age allied against our Lord and His Christ. Together, these all are employed by the dragon to make war with the Lamb and His bride in the short days that remain.

So the world is united, and in its alliance, it goes about its affairs with exclusive ends to bring all the world to unite against the Lord. John writes, "And that no man might buy or sell, save he that had the mark, or the name of the beast, or the number of his name." The number of this beast is always one short of the Lord's perfect number. What He did in six days and ended with a day of rest and glory Satan merely strives to duplicate. The number of a man is always short. It can never match the glory of the Almighty. Thus, as Revelation is set in the construct of a week, likened unto seven days, the alliances of Satan cannot duplicate the Lord's glory. Chapter 13 is all about the dragon's futile efforts in the world, with the alliances of empires and kingdoms, visible and apostate churches, and all the worlds condemned inhabitants, to try and duplicate the Lord's glory and take to himself that honor. But in the end, he falls short. Thus, the chapter ends with this acknowledgement and summation, where it is said, "Here is wisdom. Let him that hath understanding count the number of the beast: for it is the number of a man; and his number is Six hundred threescore and six." This chapter continued the story of this age begun in chapter 12. This is the final section where we find the Lord's final act of expunging His wrath and judging the world and its prince. It is the design of the Lord to once and for all deliver His bride unto the long-awaited wedding day.

Chapter 14: Babylon's Fall Heralded

The fourteenth chapter is the logical counterpart to those visions of the thirteenth chapter. What was seen was this world and its forces allied with the dragon. What is now seen is those not part of that alliance. It is a vision of the true Israel of God. It is the same one hundred and forty-four thousand seen before in the seventh chapter, but this time they are seen in allegiance with Him that has sealed them in contradistinction to those sealed by the Beast. They stand above the earth and its allied forces. We see the Lamb again for the first time since the seventh chapter, as it says, "And I looked, and, lo, a Lamb stood on the mount Sion, and with him a hundred forty and four thousand, having his Father's name written in their foreheads." The fact that He is seen on mount Sion is telling, as He stands above this world and its wretched forces. The dragon, he that is wounded, constrained, cast below, desperate, is here pitted against the one that stands above, enthroned, majestic, and high above all others. He stands with His bride, His elect, all of those from first to last, as it says, "Lo, a great multitude, which no man could number, of all nations, and kindreds, and people, and tongues, stood before the throne, and before the Lamb, clothed with white robes" (7:9). How John's heart must have been encouraged! For there, high above, majestic and enthroned stands the Lamb! And with Him is found a certain number, a definitive lot, comprised of all those of the previous age and of this last age, with Him above this earth! What a glorious image for the apostle to behold!

It would perhaps be better to include these first five verses of the fourteenth chapter with the former chapter, as it stands in comparison accordingly. The world's masses that stand with the dragon are marked and sealed by him. It is no literal mark, but the stamp of inclusion, affirmation, they stand with him in his rebellion against the Lord. They have stood with him since the days of Adam, but now join with him in one final engagement. In contrast to them are those chosen of God, the elect, true Israel, comprised of Jews and Gentiles, small and great, sealed of God, by His Spirit, having the everlasting mark of His grace. The fact that they "sing as it were a new song before the throne, and before the four beasts, and the elders: and no man could learn that song but the hundred and forty and four thousand, which were redeemed from the earth" tells us it is the song of the redeemed, which we alone that stand in Christ can know and sing.

We are found "as they which were not defiled with women; for they are virgins. These are they which follow the Lamb whithersoever he goeth." They are the virgin bride of Christ, she who in the twelfth chapter was put to flight, but promised a place in this wilderness called the world, where we flee, a "place prepared of God, that they should feed her there a thousand two hundred and threescore days." Here it says, "These were redeemed from among men, being the firstfruits unto God and to the Lamb. And in their mouth was found no guile: for they are without fault before the throne of God." Here is but the reality of this age, which has not yet reached its consummation. This is but a view of the Lord's betrothed high above this world, found in Him, full of joy and anticipation, free from the squalor and clammer of evil and fury below. We are found reigning in Him far above. As it was said in the beginning, "He hath made us kings and priests unto God and his Father; to him be glory and dominion for ever and ever. Amen" (1:6). Despite the worldly alliance just seen, we stand with Christ. How John must have smiled to see so great a comforting scene, to know that despite all the forces arrayed against our Lord and us, He shall prevail.

Chapter 14 now begins rightly with the view of

> another angel flying in the midst of heaven
> having the everlasting gospel to preach unto them
> that dwell on the earth, and to every nation, and
> kindred, and tongue, and people, saying with a
> loud voice, Fear God, and give glory to him; for
> the hour of his judgment is come: and worship
> him that made heaven, and earth, and the sea,
> and the fountains of waters.

At once the world hears the declaration of the everlasting gospel of salvation while in the next moment, it hears another angel's woeful declaration, saying, "Babylon is fallen, is fallen, that great city, because she made all nations drink of the wine of the wrath of her fornication." This herald is heard several times through this section of the text. It is that declaration that is announced as the age begins, is heralded as the war is waged, and is shouted as the end arrives. What is occurring by the declaration of three angels in heaven is an announcing of the end and futility of the earth and its alliance in this age. These three angels are dispatched in heaven to proclaim what is true on earth. Before it has come to pass it is affirmed in heaven.

We see then the first angel coming forth to proclaim the central message of this age, the message of salvation and deliverance to the once imprisoned nations; but this is a herald of warning. The nations are warned that "the hour of his judgment is come." This is the first warning to the earth below. Next, an angel proclaims the doom of Babylon, saying, "Babylon is fallen, is fallen, that great city, because she made all nations drink of the wine of the wrath of her fornication." What a remarkable declaration! Before she has fallen, she is fallen! It is as certain as done. This message will be heard again in the eighteenth chapter, but now it is proclaimed. Clearly Babylon is that nation that represents the powers that be today. Babylon not only was that Babel of Noah's days, but was that nation of Nebuchadnezzar, and is that example of the allied nations and empires of this earth that rise against our Lord and His anointed. Here the cause of her fall is proclaimed, as the beast risen from the pit of hell, instigated by the dragon, she is that earthly power of government that has ever sought to make a name for herself. She boasted in Babel, she boasted in the gardens of Nebuchadnezzar, and she boasts in our day. The angels fly forth in heaven to declare what is known above before it is done on earth.

The third angel returns our attention to the matter at hand; it is the judgment of God through the Lamb that is here the subject, as it says,

> If any man worship the beast and his image, and receive his mark in his forehead, or in his hand, The same shall drink of the wine of the wrath of God, which is poured out without mixture into the cup of his indignation; and he shall be tormented with fire and brimstone in the presence of the holy angels, and in the presence of the

Lamb. And the smoke of their torment ascendeth
up for ever and ever: and they have no rest day
nor night, who worship the beast and his image,
and whosoever receiveth the mark of his name.

What John is observing is the declarations of judgment in heaven, which shall come to pass on earth. Thus, as the gospel advances, the kingdom grows, Babylon falls, and those in that city are judged, the Lord advances in this age to victory. The world, the dragon, the beast, the false prophet, and those bearing the mark of the beast, here are seen as the declaration in heaven is sounded of their judgment. Thus, what follows is that judgment. John, the reader, and all heaven are reminded of this fact, it is not yet finished, as it is heard, "Here is the patience of the saints: here are they that keep the commandments of God, and the faith of Jesus." In heaven it is proclaimed, on earth it is advancing, as we read, "Blessed are the dead which die in the Lord from henceforth: Yea, saith the Spirit, that they may rest from their labours; and their works do follow them."

The declarations lead to a view of the end of judgment, where the Lord shall reap His harvest and bring those that remain to final judgment. An angel appears like unto the Son of Man to reap the harvest. The cloud reminds us He is from heaven, the crown reminds us of His majestic conquest, the sickle of His coming judgment. A fifth angel appears to announce the harvest. A sixth angel appears with a sickle. Finally, a seventh angel appears to announce the time of reaping, whereby we read, "And the winepress was trodden without the city, and blood came out of the winepress, even unto the horse bridles, by the space of a thousand and six hundred furlongs." In all, what has been seen are the seven angels of judgment. They begin with the gospel declaration of judgment and end with the reaping that leads to the winepress of God's wrath. Each of these angels are dispatched to announce the coming judgment. They are sent to warn the earth. What is declared follows and what will be seen is certain. As John hears and beholds these wonders, the time is set to observe the coming judgment to those forces allied below, who wage war against our Lord and His Anointed.

Chapter 15: Preparing the Angels

The fifteenth chapter opens a new vision within the last one. John says, "I saw another sign in heaven, great and marvelous," by these words the seven angels of the previous chapter are left behind. We have heard the declarations of heaven by seven angels, which, as Hendriksen says, together, "They have one purpose, namely, to warn mankind with respect to the coming judgment in order that men may turn to God in true faith" (153). The declaration of the age is judgment. This is the age of the wrath of the Lamb. Now comes that judgment. Seven angels are seen having *the seven last plagues*, which, as we have seen, are simply a symbolic way of indicating a complete and perfect judgment; contained within the scope of a week, like unto creation, it is the perfect execution of the wrath of the Lamb carried out in this present age. When one looks at the book of Revelation it is not as complex as men have made it. In fact, in full consideration it is but a grand and glorious proclamation that the Lord is sovereign in this age and shall subdue all our foes and lead us into everlasting life. We will find in the next chapter that the judgments of our Lord in this age are concurrent, variant, and executed throughout this age. Before that occurs in this vision, this chapter sets the stage for the demonstration of the execution of the Lamb's wrath in this present age to His foes.

Our first view is in heaven. We see that the sign is *in heaven*, and in heaven, there is "as it were a sea of glass mingled with fire." To understand this image, we must look to the third verse, where John writes, "And they sing the song of Moses the servant of God, and the song of the Lamb"; this serves as a key to understanding the chapter? How? Mainly, on account of the imagery behind this portion of Revelation being drawn from the image of the Exodus. As Israel once stood on the shores of the Red Sea and sang the song of Moses, so here we watch triumphant Israel sing the song of the Lamb; it is the song of victory, of the Lord's wrath and judgment, it is the song of deliverance. Thus, when we behold the *sea* mingled with *fire* it is the fire of judgment that is mingled with the sea. As the Red Sea symbolized the blood of redemption, so here the sea of fire is that which represents the furious holy zeal of the Lord, by way of the blood of the Lamb, as Hendriksen says, "It symbolizes God's transparent righteousness revealed in judgments upon the wicked" (159). This then represents what is to follow, which is the righteous judgment of the Lamb upon this rebellious world.

Here stand those that have overcome by the blood of the Lamb. It is the blood of the Lamb that brings the victory. As we read, these are gathered at the sea, "Them that had gotten the victory over the beast, and over his image, and over his mark, and over the number of his name, stand on the sea of glass, having the harps of God." Gathered together are those that bear the mark of the Lamb, who through His blood stand victorious over those of the earth, marked with the image of the beast, fulfilling that said in chapter 1, that "He hath made us kings and priests unto God and his Father; to him be glory and dominion for ever and ever. Amen." By the Lamb, through His glorious judgment, the saints above gather to sing the song of the Lamb, saying, "Great and marvellous are thy works, Lord God Almighty; just and true are thy ways, thou King of saints. Who shall not fear thee, O Lord, and glorify thy name? for thou only art holy: for all nations shall come and worship before thee; for thy judgments are made manifest." Before the image of the pouring out of the wrath of the Lamb is seen, this song is sung, just as we saw before, the final conquest of the Lamb in this age has begun and will end upon His return.

As the fifth verse begins, the scene is set, and the angels step forward from the throne of the Lord, prepared to carry out the outpouring of the pent-up fury of the Lord upon His enemies until the final enemy is subdued. The song is sung, the stage is set, "and the seven angels came out of the temple, having the seven plagues, clothed in pure and white linen, and having their breasts girded with golden girdles." That there are seven angels tells us again that this represents the full wrath of God to be poured out upon the earth and its inhabitants in this age, as seven is indicative of fullness, and endemical of a week. That they are said to come out of the temple tells us that this is the wrath of the Lamb sent forth by the sovereign decree of God; everything proceeds from Him. The fact that they are called the *seven last plagues* tells us that this is the last of days, and in them, the Lord's wrath is being expunged. As the Lord plagued Egypt, demonstrating His supremacy over the gods of Egypt, over Pharaoh, the beast, and the dragon, vindicating His name and delivering His people, so here we find that this is the age represented by those days. Here the Lamb from the throne is dispatched to execute the wrath of the Almighty upon His adversaries upon the earth. The appearance of the angels speaks to their service to the Lord, whereby His justice is pure and His majesty impeccable. The Lord's wrath is full.

The final scene of the chapter affirms this, as we read,

> One of the four beasts gave unto the seven angels seven golden vials full of the wrath of God, who liveth for ever and ever. And the temple was filled with smoke from the glory of God, and from his power; and no man was able to enter into the temple, till the seven plagues of the seven angels were fulfilled.

The four beasts reflect the glory of the Lamb. As the beast gave to the angels "seven golden vials full of the wrath of God," his doing so shows us it is the Lamb's doing. But what of the vials? The seven plagues and the seven vials, are they one and the same? In one sense, plagues are those afflictions that are administered to the earth while vials contain the pent-up fury of the Lord. In one sense, they are one and the same, but in another they are not; they are representative of the Lord's wrath and also what He brings to plague the earth. All in all, this image is clear that the Lord's wrath is readied and delivered to those angels that shall pour out their bowls upon the earth. As servants of the most high God, as those like priests tending to the service of the Lamb, they take that which is the Lord's wrath and smite the earth.

Chapter 15 then is the precursor to the certain execution of the Lamb's vengeance in this age. It is pure and holy, it is exact and relentless, it is incomprehensible and terrible, and by it the world is judged. This entire section from the twelfth chapter to the twenty-second is a grand display of the design of this age, which is to bring the Lord's judgment and wrath. The twelfth chapter began with the incarnation and left off with the Lamb enthroned and the stage set for the execution of His fury. The thirteenth chapter described the enemies of our Lord that know their days are short. The fourteenth chapter showed us the woman, true Israel, all the elect, set apart from this judgment. Then came the heralding in heaven of the six angels, spelling out and proclaiming the judgment and certain doom to those of the world below. Finally, this chapter sets the scene for the execution of the wrath of the Lamb in this age, already certain and sung of as if it had been done, but next to be detailed in full. There will be an undeniable congruence or similarity between the seals, trumpets, and bowls of the wrath of the Lord, as each provides from a different vantage the design and goal of the Lord in this last day. From the incarnation of the Lord to the return of the Lamb, this is the age decreed of the Lord from eternity past, whereby He makes war, conquering, going forth to conquer this world and its adversaries, to sum up all things, to deliver His bride complete, and to judge His enemies once and for all. This is the age of judgment. This is the age of the Lord's wrath. This is the age of our salvation. This is the age where we behold the glory of our Lord in completing all things, restoring all things, and vindicating His name. Here is the end of it all, summed up in this song, "Who shall not fear thee, O Lord, and glorify thy name? for thou only art holy: for all nations shall come and worship before thee; for thy judgments are made manifest." As John sat on the shores of Patmos, as Rome appeared unimpeded and unhindered in her fury, as the saints appeared lost, in heaven there was no cause for concern, for this was all the design of the Lord and the way to victorious conquest.

Chapter 16: The Seven Last Plagues of This Age

This chapter sits parallel to the other two visions that describe the course of these the last days. Seals and trumpets here meet with bowls of wrath. What was staged and prepared in the previous chapter is here enacted. We first hear "a great voice out of the temple saying to the seven angels, 'Go your ways, and pour out the vials of the wrath of God upon the earth.'" It is the thundering voice of the Almighty that directs the angels to act, as is indicated by it being a *great voice out of the temple.* That it says *go your ways* tells us that this action is concurrent and indeterminate. Each of the angels with the seven bowls shall pour out their bowls sequentially, as seen by John, one after the other, but as we shall see afterward, the effects of each one is overlapping and concurrent. The wrath of God is poured out upon the earth by the angels, and since the events coincide with the trumpets and seals, they are equally applied throughout this age. From the first to the last we find that this present age is the age of wrath, just as Paul said, "The wrath of God is revealed from heaven against all ungodliness and all unrighteousness of men." This is not a coming day spoken of, with plagues one after the other like in Egypt, but this is done at once, with the effects lingering throughout this age. The day is now, and it shall be done, until the voice from the throne of heaven is heard to say *it is done.*

Each angel is seen pouring out the Lord's wrath in heaven sequentially, yet the effects are not experienced consecutively on earth, they are applied *concurrently* and *particularly* throughout this age. It is as if it was done in the temple all at once, but the effects continue until the end of the age. Each vial contains a particular plague which falls upon some aspect of the earth's conjoined alliance against heaven. The image here is in the likeness of the plagues of Egypt, yet while then they were sequential, now they come to pass at a time parallel with the seals and trumpets and continue throughout time. Hendriksen says, "A very definite connecting link is established between the visions of the trumpets and that of the bowls. Trumpets warn; bowls are poured out." What John sees is symbolic, describing how and why men are afflicted in this age, all on account of the wrath of the Almighty in heaven.

As the first trumpet affected the constructs of the earth, its social customs and orders, so here the first plague falls upon the ability of men to cohort against the Lord and His own people. Remember, what John sees is thematic, in the sense that what occurs throughout this age is all from the hand of God. Where we see suffering, it is rightly due to the Lord's wrath. The bowl brings boils, which leave those marked of the devil displaced. When boils afflicted the inhabitants of Egypt, all activity ended. So here we see that the Lord afflicts those allied with Satan to hinder their united success. Mankind is afflicted in this life with misery, and we find that it is directly from the hand of the Lord; it is due to the pouring out of His wrath. Look at this world, everywhere there is suffering and misery, and all on account of sin and the Lord's recompense of wrath.

The second angel strikes the sea, indicative of mankind, where the Lord's wrath also brings death, which is upon them due to the recompense of God. The third angel plagues commerce and trade, that which men prosper from and that from which life is sustained; just as the Nile in Egypt was afflicted and the life source and livelihood of Egypt dried up, so the striking of the rivers and waters left Egypt stricken and afflicted. Equally, the Lord's wrath in this age hinders the success of men. When the fourth angel pours out his bowl and the sun is darkened, the life-giving energy and health of the sun is lost. The fifth angel strikes the kingdoms of this world. The sixth angel strikes the very life source of those kingdoms. When all is said and done, just as Egypt was stricken and left hapless by the Lord's plagues, so in this age, every aspect of living, the very livelihood of men is afflicted. Hendriksen says it well, saying, "Throughout history, especially during this entire new dispensation, God is using every department of the universe to punish the wicked and impenitent persecutors of His people" (161). In this chapter, we see the full extent of the wrath of God throughout this age brought upon the inhabitants of the earth. In this age, the Lord has purposed to plague the lives of men. If we were to ask why in this age suffering and death reign, we must acknowledge it is the sovereign, righteous act of God in judgment, the consequence of the world's rebellion.

Two undeniable truths accompany each of these plagues. First, in each and every execution of God's wrath He is vindicated as just and right. When the third angel poured forth his bowl it was said, "Even so, Lord God Almighty, true and righteous are thy judgments." The Lord is fully justified in His actions. Also, as the angels pour forth the Lord's wrath, men do not repent. When they were scorched by the heat of the fourth bowl, "they repented not to give him glory." When the fifth bowl brought darkness and pain, they "blasphemed the God of heaven because of their pains and their sores, and repented not of their deeds." Just as Pharaoh did not relent, so the inhabitants of this earth have continued to endure the outpouring of God's wrath in this age without reprieve. To the end, the world rails against heaven while the God of heaven is shown to be just. As this age is the age the Lord has sovereignly decreed and foreordained in ages past, so nothing is outside His sovereign will. This is the age in which the Lord is seen sending forth His wrath, all the while conquering and subduing this rebellious world. This is the age that the Lord is executing the fierceness of His wrath upon men, which, in the end, as it was in the days of Moses, we shall sing the song of the Lord's victory while men curse the God of heaven to their own ruin. This chapter shows us how this age is the age of the wrath of God. He has chosen to plague the earth and its inhabitants with their due reward. He does so justly, and all the while, men do not repent.

Now let us consider the details of this chapter. Observe that those plagued are those bearing the mark of the beast. The Lord's wrath remains upon them alone. The first four bowls cover the aspects of daily life, commerce, and the society of men. The fifth bowl looks to the kingdoms of this world, which are left in darkness. The sixth bowl to the source that feeds and enlivens the kingdoms of this world in abominations and heresies, false religion and lies. As the interval approaches between the sixth and final bowl, the reference is made to Armageddon. This is the day of the Lord. The coming final day. It is not a day of drawn-out battle, but a summoning to judgment for the armies and inhabitants of the world. As all Revelation is symbolic, we should not expect some elongated earthly battle at the end. Nothing stands in the way of the Lord. When Christ returns, the enemies of our Lord will simply be summoned to judgment. As this age advances, it is as if the allied enemies of our Lord are preparing for that final contest. But knowing the sovereign might of our Lord, they will not be able to sustain a fight. When the trumpet sounds, when the declaration is made, it will be done. Revelation gives no indication that the Lord's final return will be met with anything but sudden finality. Even here, there are no details of battle, merely the anticipation of it, and when it arrives, it is done.

When the last angel pours forth his bowl the proclamation is made that *it is done.* Notice the absence of any explication of a battle. The enemies are seen preparing, gathering, but oblivious to the Lord's return, as it says, "Behold, I come as a thief." Armageddon is nothing more than a symbolic representation of that place where the Lord engages the enemies of His own. Hendriksen says, "Har-Magedon is the symbol of every battle in which, when the needs is greatest and believers are oppressed, the Lord suddenly reveals His power in the interest of His distressed people and defeats the enemy."[2] Using this imagery, the sixth angel's bowl results in the hindrance of power for the Beast, here represented as Babylon, that enemy of the Lord's own, who employs every wicked deceit to mimic the glorious work of God here on earth, leading all men marked by that Beast to their own ruin. There is no indication here of some day at the end of the age where the forces of Satan unite and fight a final conflict against our Lord on earth. Rather, what is shown here is that throughout this age the wicked and all the allies of Satan are laboring without strength to prepare for the coming engagement with the Lord, but they will fail. For when the Lord returns, His sudden and unexpected return will be their sudden doom. In this age, the enemies of our Lord are preparing for that battle, but no battle will come. When Sennacherib and his army went to bed, poised outside the walls of Jerusalem, thinking they would prevail, waiting for that battle that never came, they awoke to find their army ruined and the Lord having visited them with sudden judgment. So the enemies of our Lord in this age, being afflicted by the plague of the Lord that hinders their strength, are futility preparing for the Lord's return, but His return, which shall be sudden, will leave them judged. Forget the fairytales about valleys and armies meeting in the earthly land of Israel. This sixth angel informs us that Satan's allies while preparing to meet the Lord in battle, having their strength dried, shall suddenly meet their doom. This is the age of Armageddon, preparing for that battle, which shall never come. The Lord shall return, and it shall be done.

---

[2] Hendriksen, 163.

Then and even then, shall men fail to repent. The seventh vile brings the end. It holds the end of the Lord's wrath. Symbolically the fall of Babylon, the ruin of the world and its alliances against the Lord and His elect comes. The earth is moved, the high places levelled, the structures and doings of men that had worked so long to buttress itself, prepare itself to meet the Lord, it shall in a moment fall. All that the world has prepared shall be left in ruins as the Lord is seen by this bowl's symbolism to finish His wrath. The finality of judgement will be inescapable, and it will be fierce, and it shall be sudden and complete. We with the apostle are given to behold the end, the end of the world's allegiance against the Lord. Begun at Babel, finished in Babylon, all shall fall and not prevail. For with the sudden return of Christ it will be done.

Overall, as indicated by this chapter, this is the age of the Lord's wrath being fully executed upon stubborn men, that, until the very end will not repent. The world is allied against the Lord and His elect in this age. They employ every aspect of life to subvert the Lord, social, governmental, religious, and commercial, and they do so futilely. Everything John had witnessed in his life was evidence for this. Rome would fall. Emperors would die. But the Lord would stand. As John stood upon the shores of Patmos, this he could know, that the fury of the dragon, the lust of the beast, and their armies of earthly inhabitants, would until the end engage in hostilities against his Lord, unwilling and unyielding to the very end. Yet John could look at his day and the events of it and know that all the fury and frustration of the nations and earthy men were but reactions to the wrath of God poured out upon them in this age. He could know that their efforts were futile. He could know that the day of their end was coming. He could know that the Lord was almighty and sovereign. He could know that the Lord was the one working to afflict the efforts of men. He could know that the Lord and His own would be vindicated in the end.

Chapter 17: Judging the Harlot

The seventeenth chapter continues the vision started in chapter 12 of the woman and the dragon and their present plight against the

Lamb and His Father. Here an added aspect of the dragon's warfare is afforded the apostle and the reader, involving the addition of another woman likened unto the first. Yet while that woman, the true Israel of God, the Lamb's wife, the bride of Christ, is chaste, blessed, and pure, the woman of this chapter is sullied and stained. She is seen riding upon the back of the beast. Here is pictured the allurements of this world and the world's bloodlust against us, which is saddled upon the nations. That which represents the kingdoms of this world united by the dragon, raised up from the sea of mankind, which makes war against the Lamb and His children, has a rider, and that rider is likened unto a woman; for she is seducing and seductive, and she leads men in her wake. The beast, called Babylon, representative of the empires and kingdoms that have engaged the Lord and His chosen, being the likes of Babel, Assyria, Babylon, Persia, Greece, and Rome, and all nations that follow have been but a relentless enemy seeking to unseat the Lord in His dominion and to destroy the Lord's own. Here, in this chapter, the beast is seen saddled and ridden by a whore. She is the one that is representative of the allurements of this life and the inducements of evil against the church. In all, this chapter brings into view another aspect of the world's united design against the Lord. It is the culmination and accumulation of all the forces of evil against the Lord's own.

The chapter begins with one of the seven angels that had been tasked with pouring out one of the aspects of the Lord's wrath against the forces of evil throughout this present age directing John to another view. What he shall show John will be contrasted with the similar occurrence found in the twenty-first chapter. There another of the seven angels of the bowls of wrath will take the apostle to show him another woman, the Lamb's wife, the bride of Christ. Bearing in mind this contrast, one considers that this action by the angel, since it is one of the angels that had one of the bowls of wrath, this must be a continuation of that vision begun in chapter 12. Now we, as John, are being shown another aspect of the enmity between the dragon and the Lamb. However, even more than this, this is the continued revelation of the wrath of God against His enemies. For this is called the vision of the judgment of *the great whore that sits upon many waters*. She has yet to be introduced in this prophecy, but here she is found in the wilderness of this world.

It is said that she is called the great whore, which is "she with whom the kings of the earth have committed fornication, and the inhabitants of the earth have been made drunk with the wine of her fornication." In one sense, she rides upon the beast and in another, she is seen fornicating with it and the multitudes of the nations and peoples of the earth. The woman represents all the world's enticements, its wares and stores, its treasures and pleasures, its lands and titles, its allurements and desires, which are as harlotries before all men. Rome is the perfect example of such a woman upon a beast, as she with all her comforts and prizes, all her easements and treasures, all her games and amusements, is the ultimate whore of mankind. Thus, it is said of her that "the woman was arrayed in purple and scarlet colour, and decked with gold and precious stones and pearls, having a golden cup in her hand full of abominations and filthiness of her fornication." Men have for ages been seduced by her. They have sold their souls for a night of pleasure. They have bartered away their lives for a taste of her sweetness. She is the tree of Eden, the lust of the flesh, the lust of the eyes, and the pride of life, which since the beginning has allured us and taken us from our proper place to the demise of our mortal souls. She is the great whore, and she is saddled upon the nations of this world.

Added to this thought is another aspect of the whore and her seductiveness, as she in her subtleness has enticed the kings and peoples of this earth to join with her in her exploits against the Lamb, by which in the slaying of the Lamb's own, she and they are inebriated with the blood of the saints. John had witnessed the blood lust of Rome, which turned with Nero upon the Lord's elect. He had watched as his fellow apostles had been martyred, he had watched as Rome and her emperors and kings had become inebriated by their bloodlust. This folly did not end with Rome. We find that throughout this age, the world has oft been united in fornicating with the woman in all her pleasures. We have seen that in her revelry and celebrations the whore has led the nations and empires of this world to filling up the cup of her seductions with the blood of saints. Once again, Rome stands as a fitting example of this woman as she offered the greatest of temptations combined with the murderous exploits in the slaughter of the saints; but the whore did not die with Rome. Together, the world, the beast, the lamblike beast, and the dragon, have throughout this age come to celebrate their harlotries and fornications, often making themselves drunk upon the blood of the saints.

Recalling that Revelation is thematic and not sequential, chapter 17 provides but further explication of the world in which we live. This world is united against our Lord. It is allied against His elect. This is the age in which He is conquering this world, subduing, plundering, and subjugating its forces. It is the age He oversees, directs, has designed, and sovereignly rules. It is the age of His wrath. It is the age being directed to a final end. When it is done, He shall return, and when He returns it will be finished. This chapter should remind us of Eden. It was there that Satan first put the thought in the mind of men, saying, "Has God said?" It was there that he led man to desire to *be like God.* It was there that the lust of the eyes, the pride of life, and the lust of the flesh, like a harlot led us from God. It was there that a sword was placed between us and life eternal. This chapter introduces us to the manner in which Satan in this age directs this world and its allies in blasphemy and lust.

When the angel says to John, "Come hither; I will shew unto thee the judgment of the great whore that sitteth upon many waters," notice that she is said to be sitting upon many waters. She not only rides upon the Beast, but she also sits upon all of humanity that is astir against the Lord. This is the consequence of the fall. Men have always been led away by their own pride and lust. But in this chapter, we will see how the nations and visible church are often engaged in driving us to that pursuit. Observe how the angel says that John shall see *the judgment of the great whore.* She is called great in that she has a remarkable hold upon men. This is said to be her judgment because that is what shall be shown. Notice the united culpability of all the world in their fornications with this woman, as the angel says that both the kings and the inhabitants of the earth have committed whoredoms with her. None escape her enticements. All the world and all its nations are engaged in fornication with this whore.

It is most interesting that the angel takes John to find her in the *wilderness*. The previous mention of the *wilderness* was in chapter 12:6, where it said, "And the woman fled into the wilderness, where she hath a place prepared of God, that they should feed her there a thousand two hundred and threescore days." There the woman was true Israel. Here it is the whore. She has fled to the place where the church has been said to be led. The wilderness represents this world and its ruined estate. It is the world of this age. It is here that the Lord has prepared a place of refuge for us. Here is where the whore is said to be found. She is now found sitting upon the Beast. In this age the great whore rides the Beast. It is upon the nations that the world is brought to her seductive allurements and persecutions. The fact that the Beast is *scarlot* tells us that it has made itself colored by the blood of the saints. Blaspheme is the Beast's many names. It revels in its curses of the God of heaven. The woman's many adornments are indicative of her allurements. That in her hand is found *a golden cup in her hand full of abominations and filthiness of her fornication* tells us with what she seduces and intoxicates men's minds. That upon her forehead we find written "MYSTERY, BABYLON THE GREAT, THE MOTHER OF HARLOTS AND ABOMINATIONS OF THE EARTH" simply speaks to her blasphemous design. She is the priestess of wickedness. She is the harlot mother. She has born blasphemy.

While we understand there is in history no such woman, let us remember that what John sees is symbolic. The Beast and the False Prophet are saddled with our lusts. They lead us to these blasphemous ends. There is not a nation on earth that has not been driven by pride and lust, which has not eventually found itself drunk with the blood of Christians. This is true of this age; this is the age of unification of the forces of this world to finally engage in a long and drawn-out pursuit of whoredoms. When John sees the woman, she is already drunk with the blood of the saints. How quick the world turned on the church. It wasn't a generation before Rome took up the gauntlet against us and made the blood of saints her drink. We must ask, when has this ever ceased? The age is continuously found filling with vats full of Christian blood. The fact that John marvels at what he sees is no surprise; he does not yet know and understand what he sees. Here, the angel provides the apostle with explication.

The second part of chapter 17 is a template to the understanding not only of Revelation 12–22, but also an appendix to further understanding of the basic hermeneutic of the book itself. As we saw back in chapter 1, Christ our Lord Himself established the basic hermeneutic of the book, that nothing is what it seems, by explaining the stars and candlesticks John saw. So here, the angel provides John and the reader with insight into the mysteries of the symbols. Retrospectively, the angel now explains much of what John has seen. First, John is given insight into the Beast. The Beast represents the nations of this world, as indicated by the designation that it was and is not; it is not just one great empire, it is a recurring empire. It draws its strength from hell. Its power is from the *bottomless pit*, the place where Satan has been said to have been confined. The nations and empires of this age, which are governed and directed of God, come from the instigation of Satan, and their end is perdition.

The world finds the Beast to be marvelous, and the angel explains, "They that dwell on the earth shall wonder, whose names were not written in the book of life from the foundation of the world, when they behold the beast that was, and is not, and yet is." This is the allure of life, that which brings the reprobate to blaspheme God and worship the Beast; they find the Beast wondrous—not the Lord, but the Beast. Again, the angel indicates the recurring design of the Beast saying that it *was, and is not, and yet is.* From Rome to the Holy Roman Empire, from Nero to Charlemagne, from Louis to Henry, when have men not marveled over the rule and power of nations and men.

When the angel says, "And here is the mind which hath wisdom. The seven heads are seven mountains, on which the woman sitteth. And there are seven kings: five are fallen, and one is, and the other is not yet come; and when he cometh, he must continue a short space. And the beast that was, and is not, even he is the eighth, and is of the seven, and goeth into perdition. And the ten horns which thou sawest are ten kings, which have received no kingdom as yet; but receive power as kings one hour with the beast. These have one mind, and shall give their power and strength unto the beast," the great mystery he is unveiling is the grand aspect of the Beast. Unlike the empires of Daniel's day, the Beast is a conglomeration of all those, it is a recurring empire, one that rises and falls time and again throughout this age. It manifests itself time and again in various confines of the world. This is "the eighth, and is of the seven, and goes into perdition." From Babel to the final great empire of this age the number shall be complete. Hendriksen says, "Thus, again and again the beast appears in a new embodiment. The forms change, but the essence remains throughout this entire dispensation, even throughout the history of the world until the judgment day."[3] What we are seeing is that this age is not only another in the continuation of such beasts, but the final recurring manifestation of that brought by the designs of Satan. The nations and empires of this age are but recurring occurrences of the beast.

Yet the most important part of this chapter is its end. For at the end, John is shown the futility of Satan's efforts. The beast shall not prevail. In the end it shall go to perdition. Here is the hope of every saint in this age, as we read, "These shall make war with the Lamb, and the Lamb shall overcome them: for he is Lord of lords, and King of kings: and they that are with him are called, and chosen, and faithful." The church, the true Israel of God, we His elect, while in this wilderness are pursued, downtrodden, martyred, yet our Lord reigns. The beast shall fall. The Lamb of God shall overcome all our foes. This is the most blessed of all visions, knowing that we shall prevail in Him, knowing that the wonders of the forces of our foes are nothing in comparison to Him.

As the chapter closes, a few final explanations are given to the apostle. The angel tells John,

> The waters which thou sawest, where the
> whore sitteth, are peoples, and multitudes, and
> nations, and tongues. And the ten horns which
> thou sawest upon the beast, these shall hate the

---

[3] Hendriksen, 170.

> whore, and shall make her desolate and naked,
> and shall eat her flesh, and burn her with fire.
> For God hath put in their hearts to fulfil his will,
> and to agree, and give their kingdom unto the
> beast, until the words of God shall be fulfilled.
> And the woman which thou sawest is that great
> city, which reigneth over the kings of the earth.

Keeping in line with what we have seen in Revelation, that nothing is what it seems, further explanations are given. The waters earlier in the chapter are shown to be all the inhabitants of the world, absent the elect. The horns are described as rulers. What is important here is that we find how the Lord in His providence often turns the world upon itself. For here the horns are said to "hate the whore." It says that they shall "make her desolate and naked, and shall eat her flesh, and burn her with fire." The reason is given as to why the enemies of our Lord would do so contrary an act. It is because "God has put it in their hearts to fulfil his will, and to agree, and give their kingdom until the beast, until the words of God shall be fulfilled."

God is sovereign. He directs the will and hearts of men. He at once can bring Pharaoh to stubbornly refuse Him while at the next bring him to submit to His will. Much as Amnon lusted after Tamar his sister, only to fulfill his lust in defiling her, only then to hate her, so it is with the beast and the whore. While they share a bloodlust for the saints and delight in their shared fornication, time and again nations rise up and kings against one another to carry out the will of God. While the forces of Satan should naturally delight in their common hatred, often they are found to turn on one another. This should come as no surprise. For the will and design of God often turns their lusts to hate. He often pits foe against foe, nation against nation, horn against whore. When Alaric sacked Rome, it was by the instigation and design of the Lord that Rome, that great whore would be left naked and desolate at the hands of a Vandal. Rejoice Christian, for the beast and the whore are in this age never to prevail. Time and again, the Lord brings them to ruin, turning on each other, all to their final end of perdition. As the seventeenth chapter closes, once more the reader is *blessed* to read, as was promised at the start of the book, knowing that what John marveled over was nothing to fear. For the Lord sovereignly reigns in this age.

Chapter 18: Rejoicing for Babylon Falls

The eighteenth chapter of Revelation is a reiteration of what was seen back in chapter 14, but this time, with greater detail. The fact that the fall of Babylon is now, was, and is to be, with all of its occurrences, reminds us that this is not chronological nor sequential; Babylon has fallen historically, she continues to fall, and she shall fall until her final demise. Babylon represents all those kingdoms and empires of this world allied together with the dragon, those marked with the image of the beast, along with the whore that rides upon the beast. The beast itself representing Babylon. Babylon of old, Babel, Assyria, Babylon, Persia, Greece, and Rome, which is summed up in the Babylon of Revelation, that representative force and beast of the dragon that is the enemy of Christ and His elect throughout this age. Chapter 18 shows us once more the manner and nature of Babylon's demise both now and until the end. Here begins the sequential telling of the fall of all our foes. Till now, we have seen how this age began in warfare and has continued in such hostility. Now comes the judgment of our foes. It will be told in succession, but in truth, it shall be at once in the end.

Babylon's fall is first, and it is stunning. When empires and nations, kingdoms and alliances fall, the world is startled. It is amazingly incomprehensible for the inhabitants of this world to see empires and alliances fall. History tells the tale of how often seemingly impregnable powers fell. Long ago, when the inhabitants of Babel scattered, surely the world stood amazed. When the Lord slew 185,000 Assyrians in a night, the carnages were terrifying for the world to behold. When Babylon in all her glory was no more, the world must have gasped. When Persia fell to the Greeks, surely it was never even considered possible. Yet when Alexander and his conquered world were in a moment undone, surely the world thought that empire would last forever. Still, when Rome, the seemingly greatest of them all fell to the barbarians, the world stood in disbelief. Like the fall of empires, so will the end of Babylon the Great, which represents all the forces of the earth, come with great amazement. Throughout this chapter you hear the amazement of the world at Babylon's startling end. Chapter 18 captures the amazement of the world at how unbelievable the demise of seemingly impregnable empires has been.

The chapter first begins with the utter desolation and ruin that is left when Babylon falls. As the fall of Babylon has occurred, is occurring, and shall occur, this story has been told time and again. Whenever the nations and empires of this world fall and are overrun, utter desolation is left in their habitation. God the Lord in His sovereign zeal tramples upon their lands, leaving all their comforts, fortresses, settlements, and pleasantries to the ruin and habitation of vultures. The fall of empires in history tells the story of such desolation. When Rome fell, the barbarians left in their wake a ruined empire. The pleasantries of Rome, her games and circuses, peace, and prosperity, were razed and ruined. Rome had become "the habitation of devils, and the hold of every foul spirit, and a cage of every unclean and hateful bird." The world looks on and says of the desolation, "How could this be?" As the mighty angel proclaims,

> Babylon the great is fallen, is fallen, it is further heralded that, The kings of the earth, who have committed fornication and lived deliciously with her, shall bewail her, and lament for her, when they shall see the smoke of her burning, Standing afar off for the fear of her torment, saying, Alas, alas, that great city Babylon, that mighty city! for in one hour is thy judgment come.

When empires and kingdoms fall, not only is it surprising, but it also results in the utter ruin of their once pleasant habitation.

This chapter addresses the sudden nature of the fall of empires, but not just any empire, that which represents the empires of this world, united together against the Lord, given the name Babylon the Great. When the chapter speaks of *in one hour* and *in one day, death, and mourning, and famine*, it speaks to the suddenness and inexplicable speed at which nations and kingdoms fall, but more so, how in the end, when the Lord returns, the ruin of that representing the forces of this world called *Babylon* shall in a moment be ruined. How many times in history have impregnable nations, forces, empires fallen, suddenly, as though overnight? So it is that this chapter explains not only the certainty of the fall of empires, but the fall of that called Babylon, for frail is her existence.

When the end shall come, when the Lord descends with a shout, in a moment, with but a wink, but a puff of wind, that called Babylon shall be sent tumbling. It shall come in an instant. Just as Jericho's impregnable walls fell with a shout, so shall the forces of this world fall in a moment. Babel was undone in a moment by heavenly confusion. Assyria was ruined in a night. Egypt was made desolate with a tide of the Red Sea. Rome fell in a generation. From the Spanish Armada to Alexander standing at the end of the world, no empire has lasted, and when they have fallen, how sudden was their fall. So shall Babylon's fall come in a moment. This chapter encourages us, it calls the saints to rejoice, it summons us to take comfort in the certain and sudden end of that called Babylon; thus, it is heard, "*Fallen, fallen, is Babylon the great!*" Her greatness is never but for a moment. The Lord in His strength shall send her to her ruin in an instant, as it says, for in *one hour* is she made *desolate*, and *in one hour is thy judgment come*, and *for strong is the Lord God who judgeth her*.

We also see in this chapter how the world shall stand amazed at Babylon's fall. How often have nations and peoples, merchants, and kings, been arrested in their pursuits to watch and gaze in amazement at the ruin of nations, empires, and kings. You can hear it over and again in this chapter, as the world stands amazed at Babylon's tenuous reign and sudden ruin, as it says over and again, "Alas, alas, that great city, that was clothed in fine linen, and purple, and scarlet, and decked with gold, and precious stones, and pearls!" For in one hour, so great riches have come to naught! See how the world is utterly dismayed to say, "Alas, alas, that great city, wherein were made rich all that had ships in the sea by reason of her costliness! for in one hour is she made desolate." The world that shared in the celebrations, revelries, delicacies, and comforts of Babylon the great, shall also share in her ruin. They who shared in her whoredoms, who delighted in her fornications, shall stand aloof in amazement. For how is it that she that was so glorious in a moment has become inglorious?

Meanwhile, we the saints shall stand back in awe of our Lord. We shall hear it said, "Rejoice over her, thou heaven, and ye holy apostles and prophets; for God hath avenged you on her." This chapter is not only about the world's amazement and dismay at the loss of all that Babylon represented to them, but also about our joy in the Lord's justice and our vindication in the end. She who once made herself drunk with the blood of the saints shall drink fully of the Lord's wrath. It has been declared that Babylon is fallen, and in the end, it shall finally be announced. That herald continues throughout this age. So let us not lose heart! History is but a continuous taunt to the whore and to the beast, and to the dragon himself, who despite all his seeming successes, continues to meet with sudden, certain, and swift justice from God while we watch in delight. This chapter is a fitting compendium to the sorrows of the previous chapters. It reminds us that the beast that is, was, and shall be, yet has fallen, is falling, and will fall unto the end.

So it is that this chapter ends with an echo of six taunts to the world. Over and again the phrase "οὐ μὴ εὑρεθῇ ἐν σοὶ ἔτι" or "οὐ μὴ ἀκουσθῇ ἐν σοὶ ἔτι," it *is not found nor heard in you again.* Six times over and again at the end, she that was called to rejoice, hears the taunt of the world, *never again!* Beginning with the mighty splash of a millstone violently cast to the depths, the message is heard, "That which she had, which she has, what she seeks, is cast to the depths," the millstone of her prosperity is drowned to the depths, cast with great fury to the deep waters below. All the while we stand and chant with the mighty angel, *no more, no more!* Her comforts are no more. Her celebrations are no more. Her delicacies are no more. Her circuses and games are no more. Her power, authority, wealth, and splendor are no more.

Like Jeremiah's weeping over Jerusalem, so here is the world led to weep and wail the loss of all they held dear. Their celebrations are turned to mourning. History is replete with examples of the world standing in amazement and awe at the downfall of empires, kings, and nations, wondering how it could have been. In the end, when the final stroke of the clock passes, then shall it be finally said, "Babylon the great is fallen, is fallen." Then shall the world mourn and the saints rejoice. John was afforded the privilege of watching the event prefigured in a vision, we shall behold it in the end. For now, though, while in this age the church is persecuted, slain, and pursued by the world, yet time and again, she is brought to rejoice and behold the sudden and marvelous end to those that once celebrated our demise. Fear not! Tremble not! For fallen, fallen is Babylon the great! She has, she is, and she will, and history is the tale of that ruin. History records the desolation and ruin of nations, kings, and empires, and now and in the end the Lord and His people will stand and rejoice.

Meanwhile, as Babylon falls, the whore rides to her own ruin. The nineteenth chapter begins with this,

> And after these things I heard a great voice of much people in heaven, saying, Alleluia; Salvation, and glory, and honour, and power, unto the Lord our God: For true and righteous are his judgments: for he hath judged the great whore, which did corrupt the earth with her fornication, and hath avenged the blood of his servants at her hand.

This is the consequential declaration in heaven at the events foretold in the previous chapter. There it was said,

> Babylon the great is fallen, is fallen, and is become the habitation of devils, and the hold of every foul spirit, and a cage of every unclean and hateful bird. For all nations have drunk of the wine of the wrath of her fornication, and

the kings of the earth have committed fornication with her, and the merchants of the earth are waxed rich through the abundance of her delicacies.

Remember that the beast was saddled with the whore. Together they made havoc of the church. Together, they fornicated with men and were made drunk with the blood of the saints. Now they fall to ruin together.

When Christ comes, when it is done, then shall be the end of this union. All the riches, all the delicacies, all the wonders of Babylon will be ruined, and no more shall that great whore be found. At the end we shall be delivered. Our rescue, our final salvation, is prefigured by these words, "Come out of her, my people, that ye be not partakers of her sins, and that ye receive not of her plagues." Then we shall be taken to be with Him. Then shall come the whore's great end, as we read,

> Reward her even as she rewarded you, and double unto her double according to her works: in the cup which she hath filled fill to her double. How much she hath glorified herself, and lived deliciously, so much torment and sorrow give her: for she saith in her heart, I sit a queen, and am no widow, and shall see no sorrow. Therefore shall her plagues come in one day, death, and mourning, and famine; and she shall be utterly burned with fire: for strong is the Lord God who judgeth her.

Judgment comes to the world in a moment. When the Lord returns, we shall rejoice.

This chapter is a chapter made for us to take up a taunt against the world, the whore, and all our foes. For the day is coming when the world, with all her wonders, all her merchandise and wealth listed here in the eleventh through fourteenth verse, shall be left in ruins.

Then, they who now rejoice and revel, they shall mourn while we who now mourn shall rejoice. Now, because of this chapter, we can rejoice as though it was already done. For in the end, "the merchants of the earth shall weep and mourn over her." Then shall they be like Jeremiah, saying,

> Alas, alas, that great city, that was clothed in fine linen, and purple, and scarlet, and decked with gold, and precious stones, and pearls! For in one hour so great riches is come to nought. And every shipmaster, and all the company in ships, and sailors, and as many as trade by sea, stood afar off, And cried when they saw the smoke of her burning, saying, What city is like unto this great city!

There is an echo of Jeremiah in Lamentations here. Then, Jeremiah wept as Judah was left in ruins by the ruthless Babylonians. Soon, the world shall weep and mourn in like fashion, as the world, Babylon the Great, and the great whore are no more. Then shall be heard these words, "Rejoice over her, thou heaven, and ye holy apostles and prophets; for God hath avenged you on her." The eighteenth chapter tells the tale of the coming end of the whore and the beast she rides. Likened unto Babylon, with the imagery of Lamentations, the world that now rejoices shall lament while the church shall rejoice.

With great dramatic form the chapter ends, as the angel "took up a stone like a great millstone, and cast it into the sea, saying, Thus with violence shall that great city Babylon be thrown down, and shall be found no more at all." Further woe follows, as the angel elaborates on the ruin of all the world's revelry, saying,

> The voice of harpers, and musicians, and of pipers, and trumpeters, shall be heard no more at all in thee; and no craftsman, of whatsoever craft he be, shall be found any more in thee; and the sound of a millstone shall be heard no more at

all in thee; And the light of a candle shall shine no more at all in thee; and the voice of the bridegroom and of the bride shall be heard no more at all in thee: for thy merchants were the great men of the earth; for by thy sorceries were all nations deceived. And in her was found the blood of prophets, and of saints, and of all that were slain upon the earth.

Everything that once the world transacted in shall be brought to ruins. All her wicked attempts at deceiving the nations shall be no more. In the end, all that makes up this life shall be found vain and meaningless. This chapter of Revelation is a reminder to us all of the full allegiance of the world and its ways and its united force against our Lord. We live in a world that is deluded, inebriated, given to blaspheme and hatred for our God and His elect. We have nothing and shall have nothing in it.

A lesson is taught to all the Lord's children in this chapter. We cannot find allegiance with this world. Our ways are not their ways. The angel said, "Come out of her, my people, that ye be not partakers of her sins, and that ye receive not of her plagues." We are in this world, but not of it. We are pilgrims and strangers in a hostile wilderness. The world is not our friend. We must not seek allegiances with her. Our allegiance is above. Our desires are not those of this world. They wish to be as God, we desire to be with Christ our Lord. The world does not think like us, reason like us, or have desires as we have. Revelation teaches the church of this age the certain division between the people of God and the world. We are sanctified, set apart, called to live to the glory of our Lord, knowing that the time is short. John was afforded the privilege of seeing the end, in a vision, in a dream, in symbols and figures, he was permitted to see and understand the grand design and scheme of this age. He was permitted to see from above what was actually occurring in heaven and earth; the world was not winning, the cause was not lost, Christ was on the throne, and the day was coming when we could all shout upon seeing the ruin of the forces of this world fall, saying, "Rejoice over her, thou heaven, and ye holy apostles and prophets; for God hath avenged you on her."

Chapter 19: Victory in Christ our Lord

The nineteenth chapter continues the topic previously covered; the Lord's judgment and wrath against the forces of evil in this world. The last chapter detailed the final judgment of that great whore, Babylon, while this chapter will celebrate the end to the beast and lamblike beast, heretofore called the false prophet. The harlot is cast down, the whore is stripped bare, the seductive one is overcome, and victory is found. This is celebrated at the start of the chapter. The demise of the beast consumes the latter part of the chapter. Together, we see the enemies of our Lord and His bride overcome. Add to this that which is coming in the twentieth chapter, the defeat of the devil, who is the dragon, and we shall have presaged the final conquest promised of God and of His Christ. He shall be victorious. The four hallelujahs that start this chapter sum up the chorus of heaven. As we have seen, they are celebrating the end of the great whore.

The nineteenth chapter divides into two parts. The first part covers the celebration following the demise of the great harlot. What is celebrated is the judgment of God. Four hallelujahs follow as the chapter opens. Each comes from a different source. The first is from the vast multitudes of heaven, the saints, who shout, "Alleluia; Salvation, and glory, and honour, and power, unto the Lord our God: For true and righteous are his judgments: for he hath judged the great whore, which did corrupt the earth with her fornication, and hath avenged the blood of his servants at her hand." Praise to the Lord is heralded. Praise for His salvation. Praise for His glory. Praise for His honor. And praise for His might. It is given to Him for this cause, because *true and righteous are his judgments.* Justice prevailed! How? By the avenging of the world in all her rebellion. The great whore is no more. We are avenged.

It is further announced by the masses, "Saying further, Alleluia. And her smoke rose up for ever and ever." Her end is certain and final. With this declaration comes a response. Like a chorus of heaven, the four beasts and the elders that are before the throne of God join in, shouting, *hallelujah, amen.* The final hallelujah appears to be perhaps that of all those inhabiting heaven before the Lord, said to be "a great multitude, and as the voice of many waters, and as the voice of mighty thunderings." This group is far more numerous it appears, whose voices are mighty, which, whether angels or the bride, they are heard to bring the crescendo of the chorus of heaven to shout, "Alleluia: for the Lord God omnipotent reigneth. Let us be glad and rejoice, and give honour to him: for the marriage of the Lamb is come, and his wife hath made herself ready." Perhaps it is the angels, for this hallelujah announces the readying of Christ's bride. With this great chorus then we see the end to this first act of judgment. The whore is judged. Babylon is fallen. We are delivered. And the bride is readied for the marriage supper of the Lamb.

As one can see, the understanding of this portion of Revelation is not as complex as imagined. Overall, we are observing the Lord's judgment upon a hostile world. The second part of the chapter begins in the eleventh verse. Here the heavens are opened, which has not yet occurred to this point, perhaps to best show the splendor of Christ as He is readied to ride forth in judgment. Here is first a view of the Lord in all His splendor, at first He was hidden but now He is revealed, as it goes from Him having a name that none know to the declaration that He is King of kings and Lord of lords. We first saw Him in His likeness saddled in the sixth chapter, where there He was declared to be conquering, riding forth in this age to conquer. Now we see Him again, saddled, this time followed by a heavenly host, riding forth to subdue the beast and fetch His bride. Until now, He has been orchestrating the events of this age all along, but now at the end, He comes forth to finish that work. He is said to be mounted for battle. Christ is readied to finish the war.

His appearance is now morphed. He appears as He has come to be known, as King of kings and Lord of lords. Before, in chapter 1, He was seen as an attendant priest, our High Priest. In the fifth chapter, He appeared as a Lamb that had been slain. He was seen in type in the sixth chapter, riding upon a white horse, riding forth to conquer. Now, He returns on that horse to finish the war. He comes as our King and Lord. His appearance is similar to the appearances before, but it is now changed. We now see Him as a conquering warrior, at the consequent end of His warfare, having His garments stained by the blood of His trampled enemies. Note that He alone has stained garments, not the host behind Him, as He alone subdues our foes. This age is the age of conquest, of His subduing, plundering, and wasting our enemies, from those marked by the beast, to the whore, the beast and the false prophet, and finally the devil. As He rides forth to finish His work, we find His appearance since the start of the book has changed.

The Son of God is not named in this passage. He is given titles. He is first called "Faithful and True." He is given such a name because "in righteousness he doth judge and make war." We know it is our Lord because He has the same eyes as He had in chapter 1, He has eyes *as a flame of fire*. He sees, He judges, and His judgment is true. The fact that He arrives with many crowns speaks to His conquest and exponential glory. For the first time since he wrote his gospel John hears His name as He that is called *The Word of God*. In chapter 1, the sword was protruding from His mouth, it is here seen again. Here He bears the name. It is by His word that He has conquered the nations. It is by His sovereign decrees that He has executed the fierce wrath of God, as we see that with the word, he did *smite the nations*, and with them, he "does rule them with a rod of iron: and he treadeth the winepress of the fierceness and wrath of Almighty God." As Christ appears to now show Himself as the horseman first seen in chapter 6, He now is seen coming forth to finish His work. He is to engage our great foes.

It is now that John sees

>an angel standing in the sun; and he cried
>with a loud voice, saying to all the fowls that fly
>in the midst of heaven, Come and gather your-
>selves together unto the supper of the great God;
>That ye may eat the flesh of kings, and the flesh
>of captains, and the flesh of mighty men, and the
>flesh of horses, and of them that sit on them, and

the flesh of all men, both free and bond, both small and great.

As Christ the Lord is poised to slaughter His foes upon the field of battle, heaven's angel calls the beasts of the earth to prepare for a feast of slain flesh. As though the battle was already fought and the battlefield was already strewn with the corpses of kings and captains, the beasts of the world are summoned to dine. For certain is Christ's victory. Remembering that all this is symbolic, we know that the image is of the glory of our Lord who by His word slays the nations and subdues our foes. He reigns.

Once more, just like in the previous text where the armies were said to gather for Armageddon, so here we find the beast and false prophet along "with the kings of the earth, and their armies, gathered together to make war against him that sat on the horse, and against his army." And once more, there is no battle. Instead, judgment. Their ruin is swift and sudden, as at the

> end the beast was taken, and with him the false prophet that wrought miracles before him, with which he deceived them that had received the mark of the beast, and them that worshipped his image. These both were cast alive into a lake of fire burning with brimstone. And the remnant were slain with the sword of him that sat upon the horse, which sword proceeded out of his mouth: and all the fowls were filled with their flesh.

When Christ appears, their end comes. There is no elongated engagement of forces, only judgment. The King of kings commands and our foes are cast alive unto their ruin. The end comes swift. It cannot be said enough; Revelation does not teach of some future engagement of earthly armies and rulers meeting Christ on earth in battle. Instead, it shows Christ appearing and the end suddenly coming. Here we see the end to the beast and false prophet. They join the great whore in judgment.

This does not follow one after the other. We are beholding topically the end of all the Lord's foes. First, the great whore. Now the beast and false prophet. Next the dragon, Satan himself. Last, those bearing the mark of the beast. The intent here is merely to show that all will be judged in the end. The design is to demonstrate their futility in preparing to meet Him. For He comes suddenly and they without strength are cast into eternal perdition. In this portion of Revelation, we are observing the certain end of all our foes. We are seeing that not a one shall escape their ruin. We are beholding the wonder and glory of the Lord, who when He returns will come with this new name, this certain majesty, He will ride forth with His garments stained by the blood of all His and our foes. What a glorious image for John to behold. What a wonderous truth for us to know. This age, it is the age of judgment and wrath. This world, this world is united with the great serpent, our great tempter, He who deceives the whole world. Satan and his allies are ruined. Their end is certain. They shall upon His return forever be cast into everlasting punishment. What shall we then fear? What a glorious picture to behold.

Chapter 20: Judgment of the Final Foe

The twentieth chapter of Revelation rewinds history once again back to the beginning of this age, to the first advent of our Lord. It is to detail the judgment of the dragon, the first and final enemy of the church of our Lord, our enemy from the garden to the final judgment, who here is shown to be judged already, and soon to be finally judged. Like the beast, the false prophet, and the whore before, so now the dragon, he who is behind it all, is judged. We are reminded that this is in no way chronological; John is simply detailing in each categorical area the judgment of the Lamb's foes. So having reversed the scene once again, a new aspect of the Lord's judgment begins to be detailed.

The new aspect of God's judgment here to be revealed is indicated by the words *and I saw an angel*. This chapter is remarkably congruent with the twelfth chapter of Revelation. There this final section of Revelation began in the same manner as it does here by detailing the warfare of this age between this world and heaven. It starts with the consequences of Christ's ascension to Satan in this age, our chief and principal foe. There it was the Lamb and the dragon, and all the forces below pitted against the host of heaven above. Now the focus is specifically upon the dragon.

Remember, the three divisions of Revelation which the Lord set down in the first chapter, they are the things which were (chapter 1), the things which are (chapters 2 and 3), and the things which shall shortly come to pass (chapters 4–22). Then, of the things *which shall shortly come to pass* there were three sections to be expounded in chapters 4–22. The three subdivisions of Revelation 4–22 consist of the divine sovereign decrees of God in the scroll (4–8:5), the warfare of God against this world and its forces introduced by sounding of seven trumpets (8:6–11), and this final section detailing the wrath and judgment of God against all our foes.

At the start of each of these three sections, the *things which shall shortly come to pass* rewind to the start of the age. From there, it detailed how the Lord's judgment is transacted throughout these last days until the end. Included within this final division that spans from chapters 4 to 22 were the seven bowls of judgment in chapter 16. Recall that each of the subsections of *the things which shall shortly come to pass* are the judgments of God in this age from Christ's incarnation to His second coming.

Also, recall that this age is set in Revelation in the scope of seven. It is likened unto God's work in creation. Now, the Lord's design is to perfectly complete that which was begun so long ago. This age and the coming end are seen as though it were six days of labor for the Lord and the last day of final rest. All in all, chapter 20 begins the final look at God's judgment against our original enemy, the ultimate foe, who is that final enemy of the Lord to be judged, judged not in sequential time, but in order of priority. Satan was first; Satan is last. It is Satan that stands behind the chaos and evil of the age. It is Satan that must finally be judged. From this comes the conclusion of God's work in this age and the end of this created order in time.

As stated earlier, there is a great similarity between the twelfth and twentieth chapters of Revelation. While the event detailed in both chapters is spoken of from two different vantage points, both views having two different aims, they still reveal the same event; Satan is in this age being judged, with Christ's work in the incarnation he has been judged, and ultimately, he shall finally be judged. We find the judgment of Satan begins with the appearance of Christ. His incarnation was met with the first encounter with our foe in the wilderness. His work below, His ascension above, and then, the war in heaven, all led to this fatal blow. Satan is judged, restricted, confined, and his authority rescinded. Not finally, not ultimately, nor literally. Instead, his authority is curtailed, and his influence shortened. As the kingdom of our Lord advances, Satan's sway ebbs. Thus, his blow, while fatal, is not yet final; that comes at the end. Now, he is as greatly wounded, as if confined and restricted, incarcerated until judgment falls.

Here, in chapter 20, follows the adjudication of Satan's judgment. It is he who finds his place in heaven removed. He is cast down. Again, not literally, but typically. His influence is not what it once was. And while his confining may not be spatial, but rather positional, the point is to indicate that he no longer can accuse and bring havoc to the elect, since Christ is seated as our High Priest. His blood argues against Satan's accusations. Much like the scene in Zechariah 3, he stands mute, silenced by our Advocate. By Christ coming, dying, rising, and ascending, Satan has been wounded, bruised mortally, laid low, left to pursue on earth his chaos with the time short; for his end is near. Recall that the ancient speculation of Satan's presumed fall long ago during the work of creation is not supported biblically. Rather, we see the true judgment of his rebellion beginning now with Christ having come, Satan's incremental end begins at Christ's first coming, and will end with His return.

So to make it clear, there is no coming one-thousand-year reign of Christ on earth. There is no earthly millennium. The millennium here referenced is a portrait of this age. It began at Christ's ascension, and it ends with the Lord's return. Neither is the binding of Satan literal. How can an incorporeal spirit be bound by literal chains? It cannot be. Rather, as all things in Revelation are typical, so is this passage. The detailed event here is simply that already indicated by

Revelation 12 and 16; Satan, in this age, is judged and being judged. His unrestrained authority over the nations is curtailed. It is as if he has been wounded, bound, and put in prison, awaiting the final day of his sentencing; but this is merely figurative.

Clearly, what is here revealed in Revelation 20 is that same event that was explained in chapter 12. However, this perspective is different. It is from a different vantage point. Here is told the restriction and incarceration of the devil in this age. Christ came, and having come, Satan has been chained and sealed up for the day of judgment. Remember this is symbolic. There is no literal chain, just as this is no literal one thousand years. The chain speaks to the curtailing of his authority over the nations, and the abyss is the temporary cell he is kept within until he comes forth to be judged. It is not a specific place. It is as if the Lord has said it, and in His providence and governance of this world He has limited the work of the devil. By way of the divine will Satan is as if confined.

Satan's binding occurred at the start of this age. When Christ ascended and took His seat upon the throne, when all authority was given to Him in heaven and on earth, He pronounced judgment of the devil. In John's vision, an angel is dispatched to chain and imprison the devil for this age, and while Satan continues to possess some authority during these days, his ability to wreak havoc upon the earth is not what it once was. In the previous age, he held full sway upon all nations but one. Now, he has no ultimate authority below nor access to those kept above in Christ. He is left to pursue the bride below and to finish his days in futility. He has been judged like a criminal at the bar, brought for arraignment, awaiting his final judgment and judicious pronouncement. It is during this age then that he awaits his final doom.

So with the image of a thousand glorious years, which like all time blocks in Revelation is symbolic and not literal, we find that it represents a time that is long but short; it is short from the perspective of heaven, but long from the vantage below. This is a glorious age, but a temporary one. It is the age of victory, plunder, and conquest, which is advancing to that final day of ultimate victory and judgment. As Christ said, He must first bind the strong man before

He can plunder his house. Now, He does plunder his house. He whistles to the ends of the earth, he leads captivity captive, and he leads His own from the bondage of death. He delivers us through this life, out of this abode of evil, to His rest above. There, we are said to reign in Him, with Him, free from our enemy here below. This was a glorious and comforting message for John and all first-century Christians suffering persecution and martyrdom to hear. The days are short. The age is yet victorious. The end is coming swiftly. For we are in the interim time of Christ's work, where He builds His kingdom and plunders the earth. Meanwhile, we reign in Christ above.

As this chapter begins with a rewind, a rewind back to the start of the age as well as a rewind to start of time where at the beginning our Lord and our first and greatest enemy began this plight, we should expect this to be the detailed end of Satan. Now begins the end. As first the devil is bound and confined, soon he will meet his final demise. An angel begins the chapter by descending to lay hold of the dragon, which then is bound, restrained, and confined, locked up for a time. This is the age of the beginning of the end of the dragon. In this age, his influence is curtailed, his access limited, and his place is one of confinement. He is as a criminal awaiting his moment at the bar of justice. There he shall hear the final sentence of his doom.

How it must enrage our foe to no longer have free reign over the nations, as the Lord draws innumerable numbers to Himself, plundering the deceiver's kingdom. This is not the age of loss, but of gain, not the age of defeat, but conquest, not the age of retreat, but advance. The kingdom of God is advancing, and the spoils are great. It is like the days of Joshua, wherein the Canaanite lands were invaded, set to the sword, and put to flight. So it is now, we watch as the devil knows his time is short, and as it said in chapter 12, he is greatly enraged *knowing his time is short*. The first portion of this chapter, verses 1–6, describe the nature of this age. It is an age during which the devil is confined and constrained, incarcerated by the sovereign decree of God. All the while his kingdom is spoiled, his influence is curtailed, and his doom remains certain. For as this age advances, the day of his doom draws near. So we await the sound of the seventh trumpet, when is shall be said, "The kingdoms of this world are become the kingdoms of our Lord, and of his Christ; and he shall reign for ever and ever."

Observe that the millennium involves the souls of saints not yet resurrected bodily. It occurs in heaven, not on earth. How could it possibly be an earthly millennium then? There is no earthly reign of the Lord with the saints for a thousand years, other than what we see now in the kingdom of heaven. Now we reign in Him. And while we dwell below, we are yet reigning with Him above. We are found above, reigning with Christ in this present age, not at some future point. Notice also that the millennium involves all those that have died in Christ, who but live with Him now above. Those that we saw in the sixth chapter are included in this lot, as well as all those that are sealed with the Spirit and sanctified unto the Lord. These are all those that are not of this earth and allied with the prince of this world. We are those of the first resurrection, who, when we die in this age, are caught up to our Lord and His throne above, to sit and reign with Him, awaiting the end of this age, the final resurrection.

What a glorious picture for John and the suffering saints of John's day to behold! What a glorious image for us to see! Knowing that all their brethren that have gone to the sword and the jaws of beasts are now reigning with Christ above was surely the greatest prop to the comfort of and courage of the saints. When it says, "I saw thrones, and they sat upon them, and judgment was given unto them: and I saw the souls of them that were beheaded for the witness of Jesus, and for the word of God, and which had not worshipped the beast, neither his image, neither had received his mark upon their foreheads, or in their hands; and they lived and reigned with Christ a thousand years," it speaks about this present age, where we are found absent from the body, present and reigning with the Lord. There are but two resurrections: the one of our souls in this present age, who are in Christ, and the one to come, when our bodies will be rejoined with our souls. Those who die in this age, herein called the *millennium*, are raised to be with Christ and to reign with Him above. When He returns, the dead shall arise; this is the final resurrection.

When the seventh verse begins, the end has come. Satan is loosed to draw near for judgment, with one last gasp. This is the same as that seen before with Armageddon and the seventh trumpet, it is the day of the Lord. The language is figurative and symbolic. It speaks of an enemy and his forces gathering for one final battle. This is Armageddon, that spoken of before, where on the final day, when the Lord appears, the forces of this world and their prince shall be amassed for His arrival. But as we have seen, their end shall come swift and sudden. In a moment, they shall be cast to the depths of hell forever, as it says, "[He] shall go out to deceive the nations which are in the four quarters of the earth, Gog and Magog, to gather them together to battle: the number of whom is as the sand of the sea." Once again there is no mention of a battle. The forces gather, but their end comes swiftly and suddenly. This is the imagery of the day of the Lord.

Here the Lord is employing that imagery of the days before when Christ first appeared. It was then called the day of the Lord. Its days were preceded by Gog and Magog. It was when Antiochus Epiphanies abominated the Temple before the coming of that first day of the Lord. Just as it was in that first day of the Lord, of which Malachi said, "Behold, I will send my messenger, and he shall prepare the way before me: and the Lord, whom ye seek, shall suddenly come to his temple, even the messenger of the covenant, whom ye delight in: behold, he shall come, saith the LORD of hosts. But who may abide the day of his coming? and who shall stand when he appeareth" (Mal. 3:1f), so it will be on this second day of the Lord that is approaching. It will come suddenly. The Lord shall appear. Satan shall be judged.

So shall that day come when the great blasphemer will meet his end. It shall be once more like it was when Christ first appeared. When Christ first came, Satan was poised to hinder His arrival, as we see in Revelation 12:4, "The dragon stood before the woman which was ready to be delivered, for to devour her child as soon as it was born." Satan had amassed his forces against our Lord on the day of His arrival. But he did not meet with success. Rather, he was judged and sentenced once and for all. This is what is pictured here in the twentieth chapter. When the age draws to a close it shall be as if "after that he must be loosed a little season. And I saw thrones, and they sat upon them, and judgment was given unto them." Then as

> the thousand years are expired, Satan shall be loosed out of his prison, And shall go out to deceive the nations which are in the four quarters of the earth, Gog and Magog, to gather them together to battle: the number of whom is as the sand of the sea. And they went up on the breadth of the earth, and compassed the camp of the saints about, and the beloved city: and fire came down from God out of heaven, and devoured them.

This is merely an allusion to the coming certain end of Satan, which shall come at the end of these days, and it shall come suddenly.

See with what expediency and immediacy that final day ends, as they that expire and the forces of our adversary conspire against Him and His return, just as it was during the first day of the Lord, so it shall be then, as they shall find that in a moment it shall be as if *fire came down from God out of heaven, and devoured them.* This is not a long drawn-out engagement, no great season of time at the end of this age, but this is mere imagery, which is employed to liken that day of our Lord as the day when the forces against our Lord as it once was, when they shall gather one final time for battle, only to be in a moment cast down forever. So great is our Lord that the enemy cannot prevent for a moment their own doom. The day of the Lord shall come in a moment, it shall be sudden. The battle of Armageddon is no battle, but a moment, when Satan is said to be loosed, he is loosed as it were for but for a day, a day when he cannot mount a defense against his ruin. He shall be merely summoned to the bar of judgment.

The end comes suddenly and certainly for our Lord's greatest and first foe. Recall that Revelation 12–20 details the wrath of God in this age, and at the end the wrath of God is poured out in judgment against the enemies of our Christ. This section is not chronological nor sequential; judgment does not come to the world's allies one after the other. However, this section of Revelation is recursive, where each section details the defeat of our foes one by one, rewinding each time to show God's wrath and judgment against them. It began at the dawn of this age and the end shall come in a moment. So here we find that once the devil is brought to the bar of justice, he meets his end. It comes sure, swift, in an instant, and it is final. His judgment is for ever and ever, as it says, "And the devil that deceived them was cast into the lake of fire and brimstone, where the beast and the false prophet are, and shall be tormented day and night for ever and ever."

Together, all our Lord's enemies find their final habitation in torment, where they suffer day and night forever and ever. There is found the beast, the false prophet, the great whore, and those wearing the mark of the beast and number of a man, along with our chief foe, the devil, who together with all our enemies is forever removed and judged eternal. Before the eleventh verse begins, victory is complete. The end comes and no enemy remains. Christ and His host, along with His elect prevail. The eleventh verse moves us forward to that final judgment.

Observe that the saints of God are absent from this judgment. We are in the first resurrection already with Him, and along with those of the second resurrection, our bodies are raised and united with our souls above. We sit in judgment, as we are not judged. Our judgment was in Christ, at the cross, in Him. In Him we are raised and declared just, knowing, *"There is no condemnation to those who are in Christ Jesus."* The teaching that we will one day answer for our lives as Christians is contrary to our doctrine and the clear teaching of scripture, as it says, *"Therefore having been justified by faith, we have peace with God through our Lord Jesus Christ."* The judgment detailed here in Revelation 20 is for all those that have the mark of the beast. These are those that worshipped him and bore his mark on their hands and foreheads. This judgment at *the great white throne* is that final judgment of all men that are not of Christ. The throne is white because He that sits on it is righteous and his judgments true and just.

At the great white throne, here are found all those that never bowed the knee to the Lord. They are those that then shall bow the knee to Him and answer for their crimes. It is there that they that are judged, are judged according to the sins. It is there that they have no mediator. It is there that they have no hope. Theirs is but a certain and ominous end. It is there that they pass from judgment to that place of torment to be forever united with those that they followed. It is there that those ordained to judgment and perdition, the reprobate, come reluctantly but certainly before the Lamb that judges them. It is He that they bow before, He whom they could not subdue. It is there that they answer once and for all for their hatred of our King.

As the end comes, this one and only summary judgment; there is none other. It is but one, as Hendriksen says, "The entire bible teaches but one general resurrection."[4] Here the final day is the resurrection of those that had no part in the first resurrection, as their souls have been kept in torment, separated from their bodies which lie in the ground, until this final day. Then, *death* or that state of separation ends, and *hades* or their temporary abode of suffering ends, as they are raised bodily from that former habitation, to be cast body and soul into eternal perdition forever, to a place called *a lake of fire*. Hendriksen says it thus, "Therefore, symbolically speaking, Death and Hades—now personified—are hurled into the lake of fire… Death, the separation of soul and body, and Hades, the state of separation, now cease."[5] As the beast, the false prophet, the great whore, and devil, are all finally judged and cast into the fire, so are all those, body and soul, sent to join them in the fiery lake representing hell's lasting abode. As the twentieth chapter ends, our Lord's enemies and ours are forever judged and removed from our sight. Victory is the Lamb's!

---

4   Hendriksen, 196.
5   Ibid., 196.

Chapter 21: Presenting the Bride

The twenty-first chapter continues that begun in the twelfth chapter. All along the bride of Christ has been prepared for the coming day of the Lord. Now it is said to have come. It is the final day of the Lord. It is when God's salvation is complete and our Lord's elect bride is readied. It is when the ruination of the reprobate and their leaders is done. It is then that the bride shall be found prepared for her wedding day. Here the bride is brought forth in contrast to those of the beast and his followers who are cast away. Their end was final. Their lasting abode was the lake of fire. As the angel has completed his work in pouring out the bowl of God's wrath, that now complete, he steps forth to join in and participate in the continued vision. Here, John is to see the chosen people of the Lord, the 144,000, the bride, the true Jerusalem, the temple of His habitation, His covenant ones, complete. This is to further embolden John and his readers in their plight here below. Observe that the vision is again from above, as all things good are from above. The bride, the Lamb's elect, come from above, not from the earth below.

The twenty-first chapter begins with these words: "And I saw a new heaven and a new earth: for the first heaven and the first earth were passed away; and there was no more sea." Following the pattern thus far in Revelation, we find that the sea is that formerly identified as the tumultuous mass of fallen humanity in the earth below. As the chapter opens, they are no more. They who once were tossed about by the tempest of Satan and their own lusts are found to be removed. Now there is peace, peace above and peace below. The final two chapters of Revelation are summary. They summarize the work of the Lord in salvation. They summarize the grand design of God's glory in this world. They summarize the end of this age. They detail the final admonitions of Christ to the church, as though the book finishes as it began in epistolary form. But most of all, the final two chapters of the book are given to glorify God in His salvation by parading His bride before all to see. Like the days when Ahasuerus sought to display his glory and wealth by making his bride pass before the nobles and subjects of his kingdom, so here the Lord sets His bride before all to see.

Here is the ultimate end of the glory of the Lord. It is in us who are His chosen ones in Christ. Put first before all to see "is the holy city, new Jerusalem, coming down from God out of heaven, prepared as a bride adorned for her husband." Notice Jerusalem is not Jerusalem from below, but that which it represented. It is the city whose habitation and maker are of the Lord. It comes from above. The fact that Jerusalem comes from above once more refutes any notion of an earthly place for earthly Jerusalem in the plans of God for this age. Earthly Jerusalem had its place and time in the past age. Now her place is above in Christ. Now the Israel of God are those of every nation. Now the bride of Christ is being prepared.

When it is said, "Behold, the tabernacle of God is with men, and he will dwell with them, and they shall be his people, and God himself shall be with them, and be their God. And God shall wipe away all tears from their eyes; and there shall be no more death, neither sorrow, nor crying, neither shall there be any more pain: for the former things are passed away," we find that this is due to two results; one, the Lord's completed work, and two, the removal of all our foes. Now is gone *the former things*. The warfare, the struggle, the plight of the church, gone are all our sorrows, as they are said to have *passed away*. What a joy to know that the cross is but for a moment, but our joy shall be eternal. See what the Lord has done. It is Christ of course that has completed this work. When it says, "And he that sat upon the throne said, Behold, I make all things new. And he said unto me, Write: for these words are true and faithful. And he said unto me, It is done. I am Alpha and Omega, the beginning and the end. I will give unto him that is athirst of the fountain of the water of life freely. He that overcometh shall inherit all things; and I will be his God, and he shall be my son," we are reminded of the Christocentric design of this world, this creation, and this that God has done, it is as Paul said in Colossians 1, "For by him were all things created, that are in heaven, and that are in earth, visible and invisible, whether they be thrones, or dominions, or principalities, or powers: all things were created by him, and for him: And he is before all things, and by him all things consist." As the smoke of hell clears from the previous chapter, Christ alone is once more found sitting upon the throne. It is He that has done these things.

As the book concludes, there is an abiding tension regarding what is done and what is being done. It is as if it has already been done what is being described. Yes, to an extent, we can say that now Christ has made all things new, that now God is with us, and He is our God. But not in fullness. We await the final reality of these truths. When the day of the Lord comes, when our adversaries are cast aside, when the *sea is no more*, we shall see Him. How comforting it is to reach the end and see Christ enthroned. It is as if all the chaos and trouble seen throughout the visions of the book are forgotten. For in the end, He is found and us with Him. What more could we hope for? An ominous note is found in verse 8, ominous, but comforting, as we are reminded that "the fearful, and unbelieving, and the abominable, and murderers, and whoremongers, and sorcerers, and idolaters, and all liars, shall have their part in the lake which burneth with fire and brimstone: which is the second death." They shall have no part with us.

Verse 9 begins the presentation of the bride and her abode. It continues through the fifth verse of chapter 22. We find the one to show John this final revelation is the same angel who poured out the seventh bowl. As was said earlier, that work is complete. Now he can lead John on a review of the completed work of the Lord's salvation. John sees the bride, the Lamb's wife, who comes down from above as the city of Jerusalem. Here is the final measurement of the completed temple of God. As we read,

> Her light was like unto a stone most precious, even like a jasper stone, clear as crystal; And had a wall great and high, and had twelve gates, and at the gates twelve angels, and names written thereon, which are the names of the twelve tribes of the children of Israel: On the east three gates; on the north three gates; on the south three gates; and on the west three gates. And the wall of

> the city had twelve foundations, and in them the
> names of the twelve apostles of the Lamb.

We recall that Revelation is symbolic. We recall that everything is figurative. And we remember that John is being shown that which represents the saving work of God.

The end of the Lord's salvation is that we are wed with Christ. We are wed to Him pure, chaste, and as a virgin, by way of His imputed righteousness. The end of the Lord's salvation is that we be forever united as one in love, since He loved us in Christ from before the foundations of the world. It is His design that we should be His habitation. It is a city that Abraham once longed for, "For he looked for a city which hath foundations, whose builder and maker is God" (Heb. 11:10). Just as Ezekiel had once measured the temple, just as John had earlier been called to do, so here we see the final and completed structure. It is made of the Lord, its foundation is Christ alone, and now it is complete in Him. As we look upon it, we see its glory reflected in Him. We see its likeness to that of old, demonstrating the eternal plan of the Lord's redemption. We see that it is glorious and built upon the foundation of the apostles and prophets. This is the end of the Lord's work. As each of the stones reflect the glorious attributes of our God, we see that we share in His glory in Christ. When it says, "I saw no temple therein: for the Lord God Almighty and the Lamb are the temple of it," we are reminded that this is symbolic, and the fact is that we are merely being told here that we are one with our God. There is no building, there is no city, there is no woman, these are types of the relationship we have with our God, and all because of Christ our Lord. Stand and behold the salvation of our God!

Notice that Revelation really gives little detail about our lasting abode. There is nothing here describing our life hereafter. We do read of "a new heaven and a new earth: for the first heaven and the first earth were passed away; and there was no more sea," but really, this is symbolism, demonstrating that the old order is no more. Now what? All we are told is that which is most important of all. We are told that we shall be with the Lord forever. We are told that we shall be as His beloved bride forever. We are told that sin and sorrow, death and misery shall be no more. We are told that we shall be with Him. We are told that we shall reign with Him. We are told that all our enemies shall be judged and cast to hell forever. We are told that we shall be His and He will be our God. We are told that this is His doing, that this is His work, and that we are blessed to be part of it. As Revelation comes to a close, John can return to his life and short days resting assured that Christ is on the throne and shall never be unseated. He can rest knowing that we shall never be separated from Him. He can rest knowing we reign and live with Him, both now and forever. He can rest knowing that his adversaries are and shall be judged. He can rest knowing we are victorious in Christ alone.

The final words of chapter 21 remind us of what is gone once the end comes.

> And the city had no need of the sun, neither of the moon, to shine in it: for the glory of God did lighten it, and the Lamb is the light thereof. And the nations of them which are saved shall walk in the light of it: and the kings of the earth do bring their glory and honour into it. And the gates of it shall not be shut at all by day: for there shall be no night there. And they shall bring the glory and honour of the nations into it. And there shall in no wise enter into it any thing that defileth, neither whatsoever worketh abomination, or maketh a lie: but they which are written in the Lamb's book of life.

Gone is sin, gone is fear, gone are all threats and fears. Gone are the wicked and their schemes. Gone are our foes. Gone is night and that which troubles us in the night. Gone are labors and struggles. Gone is the curse. Gone is opposition to our Mighty King. What a glory to behold.

Chapter 22
Concluding in Hope

Chapter 22 continues where the last chapter left off. It continues describing the end of the Lord's salvation. Now the book takes on a canonical form, as it completes the full redemptive design of God, as we read,

> And he shewed me a pure river of water of life, clear as crystal, proceeding out of the throne of God and of the Lamb. In the midst of the street of it, and on either side of the river, was there the tree of life, which bare twelve manner of fruits, and yielded her fruit every month: and the leaves of the tree were for the healing of the nations. And there shall be no more curse: but the throne of God and of the Lamb shall be in it; and his servants shall serve him: And they shall see his face; and his name shall be in their foreheads. And there shall be no night there; and they need no candle, neither light of the sun; for the Lord God giveth them light: and they shall reign for ever and ever.

By way of the inspiration of God, the book of our Lord is herein complete. It began with a garden. It began with two trees. It began with sin. It began with a curse. It ends with one tree remaining, the tree of life. Here is found Eden restored. Here is found the Lord's true eternal redemptive design. We now see the full scope of His glory.

Yet we remember that the book remains symbolic. The garden is but an image. The tree in this case is but a figure. In Eden, it was a tree, an actual earthly habitation with a tree. Now, we see the figurative goal of the Lord's work in this age, in both ages, which is to restore what was lost. It is His design to bring us back to that place where once a sword was seen, "a flaming sword which turned every way, to keep the way of the tree of life" (Gen. 3:24). Revelation now completes the full spectrum of scripture and the Lord's redemptive glory. This was His goal all along. This was His plan from all eternity. The river of life is that salvation Christ spoke of when He said to the woman at the well, "Whosoever drinketh of this water shall thirst again: But whosoever drinketh of the water that I shall give him shall never thirst; but the water that I shall give him shall be in him a well of water springing up into everlasting life." Salvation is here pictured. The fact that there are twelve trees, and many streets shows us that there are innumerable saints from all nations and tongues above. The whole point of this first potion of chapter 22 is to show the end of God's redemptive design. It is for us to find rest, Eden restored, and life everlasting—not literally, but in type.

From the sixth verse on the book returns to its epistolary form. It ends as an epistle, and even more, a prophecy. This affirmation, "These sayings are faithful and true: and the Lord God of the holy prophets sent his angel to shew unto his servants the things which must shortly be done," reminds us that this book refers to this age, and its design is for its use now. We can trust and believe that what the Lord said is true. Thus, we can draw from this book a worldview unlike any other. For we can believe that the nations of this world are not of Christ, but of the devil. We can trust that we are pilgrims and strangers in a hostile world. We can trust that every part of this world, from commerce to trade, governments to empires, tragedies, and troubles, are all on account of a world united against our God and His Son. We can rest assured that Christ now reigns. We can believe that the Word of God is the weapon of our Lord's conquest, which by His blood He defeats our foes. We can believe that we are now conquerors, kings and priests, those that are His beloved, soon to be united with Him. We can trust that He is sovereign in all things, that all things work together for good for those of His love, and that the enemy brings upon itself its own ruin. We can believe that all things shall be recompensed to those to whom it is due. We can trust that this is the final age, of which there are but two, and that He shall return in a moment, and then it shall be done.

Thus, Jesus says, "Behold, I come quickly: blessed is he that keepeth the sayings of the prophecy of this book." Three times Jesus will say this, in verses 7, 12, and 20, reminding us that now these things are at hand and at any moment He may appear to roll up heaven and earth. There will be no special signs, there will be no earthly millennium, there is no single nation or empire, ruler or antichrist, but in the end, He shall appear and then shall come to pass this saying, "Death is swallowed up in victory. O death, where is thy sting? O grave, where is thy victory? The sting of death is sin; and the strength of sin is the law. But thanks be to God, which giveth us the victory through our Lord Jesus Christ" (1 Cor. 15:54f). When John falls before the angel to worship him, we are reminded just how incomprehensible and glorious this revelation was for the man; it is hard enough for us to imagine. But John was overwhelmed, reminding us that we are but flesh. There is a heaven and a place beyond our comprehension and imagination. Let us remember we are but flesh. Perhaps it is best to remember the angel's words to John, *Worship God.* This is the best directive of the book. We must behold these things and be led to worship God. For He is sovereign and just, holy and immense, and His ways are not our ways.

When our Lord says, "Seal not the sayings of the prophecy of this book: for the time is at hand," we are reminded of what was stated at the beginning of this exposition. Many have misconstrued or ignored this book. It can no longer be ignored. It can no longer be misinterpreted. It is vital that we understand this book and put it to use. It is the one book of scripture that defines and describes this age. It is the one book of scripture that affords us a grand and broad understanding of the Lord's sovereign design of this age and the age before. It is the book that can provide us with a right view of living in these last days. We must understand the world we live in. We must understand our foes. We must understand that the world is not our friend. We must understand that there is no Christian nation. We must understand that the types and shadows of the Old Covenant are no more. We must understand who are those that are the true Israel of God. We must understand that now is the day of the Lord's wrath and reign. We must understand that when Christ returns it is done, there shall be no other days, no other millennium, no other scheme or time, but the day of the Lord will come suddenly and then the end. Thus, the Lord's admonition, "He that is unjust, let him be unjust still: and he which is filthy, let him be filthy still: and he that is righteous, let him be righteous still: and he that is holy, let him be holy still." The time is now, the time is short, He shall come quickly.

The book ends as it began with a final view of our Lord, saying,

> I am Alpha and Omega, the beginning and the end, the first and the last. Blessed are they that do his commandments, that they may have right to the tree of life, and may enter in through the gates into the city. For without are dogs, and sorcerers, and whoremongers, and murderers, and idolaters, and whosoever loveth and maketh a lie. I Jesus have sent mine angel to testify unto you these things in the churches. I am the root and the offspring of David, and the bright and morning star. And the Spirit and the bride say, Come. And let him that heareth say, Come. And let him that is athirst come. And whosoever will, let him take the water of life freely.

We are left with a reminder to holiness. We are left with a reminder of the imperative of the day. Christ the Lord authenticates the book. He affirms the divine nature of it. As He leaves us with all the titles of His glory that remind us of His eternal work, we are reminded of the imperative of the day. We are to watch for His return; we are to be ready.

As Revelation began with several introductions, so it ends with several conclusions. First, the angel completes showing John of the things that shall be. Then, Christ affixes the book with the stamp of His authority, approval, and urgency. Finally, John joins in to affirm not only the urgency of the message, but also the certainty of Christ's return. Joining in with the chorus we agree with Christ our Lord, saying, "Come. And let him that heareth say, Come. And let him that is athirst come. And whosoever will, let him take the water of life freely. By the Spirit, of the Spirit, with our Lord we affirm this exhortation; Come!" One glaring note concludes this prophecy and that is the plea for Christ to come. For by coming, all shall be done.

How the last four verses fit into these concluding admonitions is uncertain. Whether it is Christ completing His words or John taking up the conclusion is uncertain, it could be Christ, it could be John, or it could be both in agreement, saying,

> For I testify unto every man that heareth the words of the prophecy of this book, If any man shall add unto these things, God shall add unto him the plagues that are written in this book: And if any man shall take away from the words of the book of this prophecy, God shall take away his part out of the book of life, and out of the holy city, and from the things which are written in this book. He which testifieth these things saith, Surely I come quickly. Amen.

It is best to think that Christ is the one affixes this warning to the book, thus leaving these few and final words to John, "Even so, come, Lord Jesus. The grace of our Lord Jesus Christ be with you all. Amen." It is not only probable, but certain that it is the Lord that threatens those that corrupt His word, as He alone has the authority and power to carry out such a sentence.

Thus, John has but few and brief words as Revelation concludes, he joins in the chorus of those along with Christ our Lord that say, "Even so, come, Lord Jesus. The grace of our Lord Jesus Christ be with you all. Amen." What is Revelation then? It is a book about this age. It is a book about the sum of all ages, the former days, and these last days. It is a book that lays out the eternal redemptive plan of God in Christ by the Spirit in these final days. It is the book that through symbols and images displays the reality of this life, the nature of this world, the way of all things. It describes the grand and glorious mystery of godliness and holiness, of mercy and justice. It is a book that rightly and perfectly caps the whole of God's special revelation through His Son by inspiration of the Spirit. The last living witness of our Lord's life is here called to complete the work begun by Moses so long ago. He leaves us with the perfect and complete, sufficient and efficient, incomparable and glorious word of the living God, of which none more be needed. For it completely finishes the story. It is not a book about future times and ages, it is not a book of mere speculation for today. It is a book that truly blesses the reader, that provides comfort, peace, and felicitous hope, knowing that our Lord reigns and we reign with Him. How could we conclude a study of this book? Merely by saying as John in closing the prophetic epistle, "Even so, come, Lord Jesus. The grace of our Lord Jesus Christ be with you all. Amen."

EPILOGUE

How then might this author clarify the book of Revelation in short terms? First, one might approach the clarity of Revelation negatively. There will be no one-thousand-year earthly reign of Christ; that is but a figurative way of speaking of his reign over this earth for this age. There is no one person called Antichrist, for it is but a term applied to those within the visible church that are opposed to Christ. It is the lamblike beast best represented by the Holy Roman Church, an apostate, evil dominion ruled by Satan himself. There will be no earthly battle of Armageddon, for it is but a type of the opposition found on earth when Christ returns. It is a battle that will never be fought, for with but a word the Lamb shall slay his enemies upon his appearing. There will be no rapture, for the church is here, ever-present during this age. And this age is the last and final age; there shall be no more preceding the restoration of all things.

There will be no great tribulation; but while there will be times of great tribulation, still this age is an age of great tribulation as the persecuted woman, the church, known as Israel awaits her King's return. There will be no numbered people in heaven nor upon the earth totaling 144,000 actual people as the number does but represent all the elect from the previous age to the end of this age. It is the perfect accounting of the complete bride of Christ, the sheep of the sheepfold, the elect in total. Revelation is not a complicated book. It is not intended to confuse us. Nor is it a book of an imaginary age intended for another day. It is the last and final book the Lord gave us for this age. It is the end of the story. It is the book that we have for hope, to cherish as the days linger, to sustain the bride of Christ until the coming day of the Lord.

So from a negative perspective, Revelation is not what so many believe it to be. It is but a book that describes God's grand design for this age. It is the end of God's revealed word for all ages until the end. It is the final declaration of His will until Christ's return. An analysis of the design and intent of the book of Revelation within the scope of God's redemptive work and eternal plan, as it relates to the whole of the canon of Scripture, leaves us with an undeniable conclusion: Revelation is God's last word of the ages. We may expect none other.

Furthermore, one might say that Revelation is the follow-up to Daniel or that it is the Daniel of the New Testament, the book illustrating the grand overview of God's sovereign work in this age, from first to last, whereby with Christ upon the throne, ruling the kingdom of heaven and advancing to conquer the nations, God is completing his eternal plan. This is the final age. It is the fulfillment of the first and a compendium of the last. It is the book illustrating the age in which the Lord is bringing all things to their end. It makes known His purpose from the beginning, which is now reaching its culmination. The age will end with Christ's return. It will end with the final judgment of the Lamb. It will end with the bride of Christ delivered to her groom. It will end with paradise restored but restored to far greater glory than before.

While the first age was the age anticipating this age, the age of types and shadows, it was the age of anticipation for the promised seed. It was the age of hope, whereby from Adam onward, all the saints of God, and creation itself, were awaiting the hidden mystery of redemption by way of the promised seed. It was Christ that was to come to redeem that which was lost. It was the age anticipating the Lord who was to come, who would save His people from their sins. He came and overcame the world. As He has gone, He has left the Spirit as the seal of His promise. This is the age of the Spirit of God. It is the age of fulfillment. Gone are types and shadows. Gone are sacrifices and earthly priests. Now Christ reigns. He is now orchestrating the final directives of the Father in this present age to bring about the conquest of the world and to fetch and deliver His cherished bride.

Yet this age is quite like the former age. It is an age in which God sovereignly rules and directs all things after the counsel of His will. Revelation is the book to set forth the plan of God for this present age. As shown, this age is set forth in three parts: the unveiling of the eternal plan of God as seen in the seven seals, the riding forth of God's will in Christ to conquer and subdue the nations, and the judgment of Babylon and gathering of the elect. All this is God's eternal plan. It was what He determined to do before even laying the foundation of the world. His people can rest assured of these things, then knowing that all things that come to pass in these days are orchestrated by the sovereign hand of God, knowing that every twist and turn of life is the Lord moving and directing all things for good for those loved of God, as He brings judgment upon the earth and deliverance for His own. In the end, as the final day advances, the echo of Christ at the end of Revelation can be heard as he says, "Surely I come quickly."

It will come without warning. It will come without sign or indication. It will be as it was in the first world before the flood or like it was in the days of Sodom and Gomorrah. The world will be about its wretched business while the saints of God eagerly long for His coming. So we wait! The church sits eager, yearning for the breaking dawn, hoping to see the heaven's rent and the Lord descend in a chariot, bringing salvation and the end once and for all of our troubles. It will be in a moment. It will be finished in an instant. Then once and for all, it will be done. Whatever day the Lord has chosen, no man can know; no man shall know. Simply, let the bride wait. Let the Lord come. And let the book of Revelation be used of the church, cherished by the saints, and no longer used for pathetic fables and foolish fancies. Let it be the book of a majestic form but a clear and simple message. This world is the Lord's; His will is being done. He is conquering the nations, judging them, and bringing about our final salvation. Let all the saints of God say, "Come!"

SELECT BIBLIOGRAPHY
OF COMMENTARIES
CITED OR CONSULTED

Baugh, S. M. A New Testament Greek Primer, 2nd ed. Phillipsburg: P&R Publishing, 2009.

Calvin, John. *Calvin: Institutes of the Christian Religion, The Library of Christian Classics, Vol. XX.* Philadelphia: The Westminster Press, 1960.

Duguid, Iain M. *Daniel.* Reformed Expository Commentary: A Series. Phillipsburg: P&R Publishing, 2008,

Durham, James. *A Commentary upon the Book of the Revelation.* Willow Street: Old Paths Publications, 2000.

Hendriksen, William. *More Than Conquerors: An Interpretation of the Book of Revelation An Interpretation of the Book of Revelation.* Grand Rapids: Baker Books, 2015.

Kuhn, Karl Georg ed. Kittel, Gerhard, Bromiley, Geoffrey W., and Friedrich, Gerhard *Theological Dictionary of the New Testament.* Grand Rapids: Eerdmans, 1964.

Louw, Johannes P. and Nida, Eugene Albert. *Greek-English Lexicon of the New Testament: Based on Semantic Domains.* New York: United Bible Societies, 1996.

Ramsey, James. *Revelation: An Exposition of the First 11 Chapters.* Geneva Series of Commentaries. Carlisle: Banner of Truth Trust,1977.

ABOUT THE AUTHOR

K. D. Hartley (ThD, Biblical Institute of Franklin, Tennessee, of the Lesser Antilles; PhD (ABD) Westminster Theological Seminary; MDiv, Chesapeake Theological Seminary; MA, Liberty University; BA, Saint Leo College) is an ordained pastor of thirty years, presently serving as the senior pastor of Good Shepherd Presbyterian Church in Ajo, Arizona. He is an adjunct professor of theology at Grand Canyon University in Phoenix, Arizona. He has four children and grandchildren and is married to Oneida, his wife of thirty-eight years.